Black American Literature and Humanism

Black American Literature and Humanism

R. BAXTER MILLER
editor

THE UNIVERSITY PRESS OF KENTUCKY

Publication of this book was made possible in part by
a grant from the University of Tennessee Better English
Fund, established by John C. Hodges.

Library of Congress Cataloging in Publication Data

Main entry under title:

Black American literature and humanism

　　Papers from a conference held Nov. 30-Dec. 1, 1978,
at the University of Tennessee, Knoxville.
　　Includes bibliographical references.
　　1. American literature — Afro-American authors —
History and criticism — Congresses. 2. Humanism in
literature — Congresses. 3. American literature — 20th
century — History and criticism — Congresses. I. Miller,
R. Baxter.
PS153.N5B53　　　　　810'.9'896073　　　　　80-5179
ISBN 0-8131-1436-5

Editorial and Sales Offices: Lexington, Kentucky 40506

Contents

Preface

Professor Charles H. Long, Visiting Scholar of Religion, recently lectured at the University of Tennessee, Knoxville, on the need to reconstruct the meanings of primitivism and civilization. The process, he advised, would enhance the definition of humanism. With his help, I understand more deeply the success of a recent conference on Black American Literature and Humanism. The American Council of Learned Societies and the John C. Hodges Better English Fund financed the meeting, held November 30–December 1, 1978. Originally I intended to examine the way that scholars use Black American literature to train American humanists in the "classical sense." The professors attending would have learned to "minimize any discrepancy between human action and the highest value reflected in the arts." Even the well-meant prospectus, however, suggested that traditional norms, cultural values, and manners were fixed. The conference papers, rather, show the importance of enriching and enlivening the standards.

Demonstrating a wide range of critical approaches, this book represents a pluralistic methodology. Seven essayists cover several literary genres and theoretical problems. Alice Childress and Michael S. Harper illustrate humanism in their writings. Richard K. Barksdale places Langston Hughes's folk poetry in literary history, and George Kent discusses the aesthetic values of Gwendolyn Brooks's folk world. Trudier Harris examines the translation of folk conventions into the humanistic fiction of Sarah Wright, Alice Walker, and Paule Marshall. As a practical reader, I demonstrate a theory of humanism informing Brooks's poetry. Chester J. Fontenot, rather, offers a hypothesis for integrating pure formalism with cultural criticism.

The final proposal to ACLS read, "The purpose here is not to abolish diversity but to emphasize commonality."

I still want to complement history, morality, and sociology with formalism, psychological criticism, myth, and reader response. I hope, as well, to improve the sophistication of a Black Aesthetic, whose major theorists have been Addison Gayle, Jr., Maulanga Karenga, Hoyt Fuller, Carolyn Fowler, Jerry W. Ward, Jr., and Houston A. Baker, Jr. While acknowledging the historical and political influences upon Black American literature, the papers gathered here explore audience and technique. They show the cultural values which help to shape the aesthetic work and which contribute to the assessment. Extending the possibilities of Anglo-American literature, Black American writing ironically recreates and modifies the tradition.

I acknowledge my indebtedness to Jessica G. Miller for advice on the original proposal. Both Donna Walter and Gloria Johnson provided valuable insights into the poetry of Gwendolyn Brooks. I also thank Carolyn Stinnett, a meticulous typist-editor. Charles H. Rowell kindly recommended the manuscript to the University Press of Kentucky, where Kenneth Cherry provided firm direction as well as encouragement. The anonymous readers of the submitted manuscript offered excellent advice. Equally important were the contributors of essays whose serious commitment to scholarly quality strengthened my purpose. No amount of thanks can express my gratitude to John H. Fisher, who showed keen interest and helped to win essential support from the American scholarly community. Finally, I thank the American Council of Learned Societies and the Better English Fund, established by John C. Hodges, for subsidizing publication.

R. BAXTER MILLER

*Knowledge counts only if it
enhances self-understanding,
if it deepens and broadens
the image of human life.*

R. BAXTER MILLER

Introduction

How does one relate Afro-American literature to humanism? The reader must realize, first, that the term
humanism is complex historically; second, that the oppositions set against it are largely contrived;[1] third,
that the New Humanists of the 1930s distorted the high
purpose of the philosophy into a conservatism which indirectly encouraged bigotry; and fourth, that the essays
collected here suggest the possibility of freeing scholarship from Western culture's self-imposed restrictions.
In the reopened range of human effort, Black literature
has dignity and meaning.
    Where does humanism begin? Hadas, like many schol-
ars, traces the idea to Greece in the fifth century
B.C., and specifically to Pythagoras, the philosopher
and mathematician who formulated the doctrine of man as
center of all things.[2] More recently, Edgar Pierce,
professor emeritus at Harvard, associated the movement
with the idealized man of twelfth-century Europe.[3]
Others place the beginnings of humanism mainly in the
European Renaissance of the sixteenth and seventeenth
centuries.[4] Few associate humanism with humanitarianism, an analogy which is more modern than historical.
Although some educators see humanism as opposing science, Pierce views Galileo as a humanist who relied upon the senses rather than upon the scriptures. Irving
Babbitt, formerly a professor at Harvard, defines the
movement as "the exchange of ideas regarding those aspects of life that fall outside the merely quantitative
and material."[5] For others, humanism sets man against
nature and self-determination against determinism.
    Modern humanism in the United States has been shaped

by the New Humanists of the 1930s. Most were connected
with Harvard, either as professors or as students. Em-
phasizing gentility, they condemned American naturalism
as a "barbaric" style. With Thomas Jefferson, they fa-
vored a natural aristocracy over an open democracy. In
Harvard's Department of Comparative Literature, Babbitt
taught, at various times, John Sherman, Norman Foerster,
and T. S. Eliot. Although Eliot was only a partial af-
filiate, Babbitt's major student antagonists were Van
Wyck Brooks and Walter Lippmann. Criticizing Rousseau
and romanticism, Babbitt sought the recovery of human
law, self-discipline, and traditional moral values. His
student John Sherman, educated first at Williams and
later at Harvard, disapproved of German culture in 1918,
but called the allies the "whole family of civilized nations." Frowning upon Theodore Dreiser, Sherman praised
Emerson and Hawthorne as illustrating useful directions
for man's spiritual fulfillment and self-mastery. These
writers, he thought, showed the distinctly human qualities, and he found democratic humanism in Whitman as
well as in Twain. By then Norman Foerster had already
studied with Babbitt. First an undergraduate at Harvard, Foerster did graduate work both there and at Wis-
consin, and later became professor of literary criticism
and romanticism at the University of North Carolina at
Chapel Hill.[6] All considered, the group converted means
into ends. Cultural value, for them, opposed a curriculum which made electives possible, since law took precedence over spirit. Yet how do rules transcend ideals?
Does tradition legitimatize values? Do values, rather,
legitimatize tradition? Answering "yes" to tradition
alone, the New Humanists avoided talking about the lower
classes, the subject of much naturalistic fiction. For
them, its characters lacked those genteel qualities
which justified human existence.

Paradoxically, the New Humanists seriously threatened
knowledge, for their closed system excluded the modernism of Joyce, jeopardized an expanded curriculum in education, and undermined the romantic tradition. Their
major weakness was to place humanness in the past, to
reduce diachrony to synchrony, and to make classical
"order" and "culture" ultimate values. Babbitt wrote:
"It is self-evident that humanitarianism of the scientific or utilitarian type, with its glorification of the

specialist who is ready to sacrifice his rounded development, if only he can contribute his mite to 'progress,' is at odds with the humanistic ideal of poise and
proportion."[7] But here his tone differs subtly from
that of the early humanists. "Poise and proportion"
suggests that Babbitt views style and manner as occur-
ring in a purely objective world. Even Pythagoras,
however, suggested that the humanist uses the self to
interpret reality. Whereas in Babbitt's system humanism
is inert, in Pythagoras' it is dynamic, since life and
will imply mental activity.

Paul Elmer More, another New Humanist, was similarly
reactionary. Having remarked on Joyce's "drab realism,"
More criticizes Whitehead's *Science and the Modern
World*. Whitehead had contended that modern man's fu-
tility results from an inability to reconcile scientific
realism with self-determination, but More replies that
hopelessness comes from making the effort.[8] Yet More's
recitation stands out:

> There are two lovers discrete
> Not reconciled —
> Law for man, and law for thing;
> The last builds town and fleet;
> But it runs wild
> And doth the man unking.[9]

On one level the poem separates body from spirit, and on
another it divides the aristocracy from the peasantry.
In contrast, Gwendolyn Brooks's long poem "The Sundays
of Satin-Legs Smith" portrays a Black folk character:

> You might as well —
> Unless you care to set the world a-boil
> And do a lot of equalizing things,
> Remove a little ermine, say, from kings,
> Shake hands with paupers and appoint them men,
> For instance — certainly you might as well
> Leave him his lotion, lavender and oil.[10]

Just as the first poem celebrates the king, the second
elevates the common man, enlarging the definition of
humanness. More's speaker differs from Brooks's primarily in equating social class with human value.

Intolerance comes from associating humanism with a
particular class and its manners. When outlining the

qualities of humanism (learning, imagination, and sympathy), Edgar Pierce finally mentions "civility." Almost self-consciously he admits, "through accidents of origin this was the code of the gentleman and the courtier."[11] Howard Mumford Jones, lecturing during the riots of the 1960s, described patience and responsibility as desirable virtues for a scholar. Violence, he said, disrupts "order" and "culture." Where culture becomes fixed, singular, and absolute, Richard Wright's *Native Son* becomes, for Jones, a one-dimensional book celebrating violence.[12]

In a deeper reading, however, that novel tests the assumptions of the European and American romantics. By portraying Black life in a Chicago ghetto, it illuminates the protagonist's ontological world. Wright's theme goes back to Hawthorne's *Marble Faun,* Dostoevski's *Crime and Punishment,* and Milton's *Paradise Lost.* For Bigger Thomas, Wright's hero, the laws are inhumane because emblems imperfectly express ideals. Ultimately Bigger seeks self-awareness, and he discovers that the basis of law lies in conscience. Even so, law remains. *Native Son* illustrates a quest for a better self and a better world. Why offer a reading at such length? The book compels the traditional reader to broaden the image of humanness.

The New Humanists hardly saw either literature or education in this way. More characteristic was a Yale professor who argued that state schools could train America's body — fertilizer and railroad men — while the Eastern schools saved its soul.[13] Class superiority easily became moral transcendence. Even Babbitt's student John Sherman had to resist that idea, although he stood almost alone among the New Humanists in doing so. Norman Foerster, in contrast, conceded that "even the slowest minds might pick up a little culture on the way through [the university] but that was a small return for the toll exacted on the superior students." At the same time, Nicholas Murray Butler of Columbia sadly viewed the loss of the simple profession of gentlemen, "the general and reflective use of leisure." He feared the football, the automobile, and the hustling scholar. J. David Hoeveler, Jr., explains: "The Humanists' discussion of education indicates as well as any other subject their alienation from the American mainstream. Their

aspirations in education were elitist and aristocratic
in the face of the democratic tide. Babbitt, More, and
Foerster could never see what Sherman recognized as
true: that no effective democracy can ignore the broad
mass of its people." Hoeveler sympathizes with the
scholars who "feared greatly for the survival of cultural values."[14] But what values should last? The New
Humanists realized that literature influences ethics.
They knew that the literary reader participates in an
aesthetic experience, and they understood well that
artifacts both reveal and shape culture. The ignored
question, however, was whether the scholar would shape
broadly or narrowly.

When Allen Tate and T. S. Eliot combined with the
southern agrarians of the late 1920s and early 1930s,
the answer clearly appeared. Stressing tradition, reason, and authority, the group avoided free-thinking Jews
and Blacks. Especially in the 1930s, they contributed
heavily to Seward Collins's fascist *American Review*. As
one story goes, Babbitt joked with his academic friend
G. R. Elliot about a Phi Beta Kappa meeting at which
Babbitt and the well-known president of a university had
been invited to speak. Following the president's discussion on "The Value of Ideals," the professor spoke
about "The Value of Standards as Opposed to Ideals."
Although Babbitt pleased himself, questions are likely.
Without ideals, how do standards exist? Do norms survive independently of consciousness and will? Can judgments inevitably erode the ideals which justify them?
Such standards lack validity. Especially over the last
forty years, major ethical thinkers have shown the contradiction in equating Christianity with cultivation and
refinement. Even a well-meaning scholar such as Jacques
Maritain says, "Humanism is inseparable from civilization and culture, these two words being taken as themselves synonymous."[15]

The seven papers collected here contribute signifi-
cantly to modern scholarship and criticism because they
define humanism from an Afro-American perspective. They
meaningfully reveal a mutual influence. Black scholars
and writers identify with the humanity of Black characters, and the characters project an ideal reader, a cultural confidant, who must share that bond. The reader
merges with the writer, as the latter reopens the range

of values. George Kent and R. Baxter Miller hold that
Gwendolyn Brooks's poetry illustrates and illuminates
the effort; Richard Barksdale shows that Langston
Hughes's personae maintain it despite defeats and dis-
illusions. Michael Harper observes the writer's "antag-
onistic cooperation" in literary tradition (some Harold
Bloom here?), just as Alice Childress views the author's
paradoxical complicity with technology. Trudier Harris
expresses the tension in a symbolic line which separates
the church from the folk.

What methodology can simultaneously evaluate author,
society, and artifact? To answer, the humanist must
combine object and experience in an act of "total perception." Reaffirming ethical values, scholars and artists read the qualities back into their literature. But
the return comes only by conceding an identity in race
and culture. Humanism is not a tradition; it is the
medium through which all traditions exist.

----

[1]Against humanism have been set medieval theology, eigh-
teenth-century reason and logic, nineteenth-century science,
twentieth-century science, naturalism, and social science.

[2]Moses Hadas, *The Greek Ideal and Its Survival* (New York:
Harper and Row, 1960), p. 101.

[3]Edgar Pierce, *The Humanity of Man* (New York: Braziller,
1956), p. 5.

[4]Norman Foerster, ed., *Humanism and America* (New York:
Farrar and Rinehardt, 1950); Corliss Lamont, *Humanism as Philosophy* (New York: Philosophical Library, 1949); J. A. C. Fag-
gonier Auer, *Humanism vs. Theism* (Yellow Springs, Ohio: Antioch
Press, 1951).

[5]Irving Babbitt, "Humanism: An Essay on Definition," in
Foerster, *Humanism and America,* p. 25.

[6]The New Humanist movement is traced by J. David Hoeveler,
Jr., in *The New Humanism* (Charlottesville: Univ. of Virginia
Press, 1977).

[7]Babbitt, "Humanism," p. 31.

[8]Paul Elmer More, "The Humility of Common Sense," in Foerster, *Humanism and America,* pp. 63-64.

[9]Ibid., pp. 73-74.

[10]Gwendolyn Brooks, "The Sundays of Satin-Legs Smith," *The
World of Gwendolyn Brooks* (New York: Harper and Row, 1971),
p. 27.

[11]Pierce, *Humanity of Man,* p. 50.

[12]Howard Mumford Jones, *Violence and the Humanist* (Middlebury, Vermont: Middlebury College, 1967), p. 17.

[13]Hoeveler, *New Humanism,* p. 115.

[14]Ibid., pp. 117, 118, 112, 123.

[15]Jacques Maritain, *True Humanism* (London: Geoffrey Bless, 1938), p. xiv.

ALICE CHILDRESS

Knowing the Human Condition

Many playwrights today extend efforts into mass media
where they reach a greater audience, but the freedom of
topic and treatment becomes more restricted. A flood
of television tape and motion picture film washes forth
subjects ignored in the past, such as drug addiction,
sadomasochism, and mental illness, but all too often the
result becomes an unfortunate and relentless attempt to
make sex and violence the most popular themes. We are
commercially deluged with community and national disas-
ters which capitalize on fright, horror, and supersti-
tion, even though no ghost creates the evils haunting
us individually and socially. Neither a werewolf, a
vampire, nor any "creature" from the deep or from outer
space is responsible. We cannot truly blame any of the
unknown forms and shadows which make us shiver and shake
for entertainment as we "enjoy" a "good" murder.

Popular forms are "Earthquake," "Jaws," and the many
other titles which tell of shipwrecks, floods, fires,
and atomic cataclysms. Many of these stories project
things to come. Any extraterrestrial being, any alien,
appears ugly, vicious, and threatening. Earthlings are
presented as the superior creatures in the universe.
They (we) must plan to defeat all other worlds and rule
any form of life throughout endless space. The imagery,
of course, reflects our home-grown bias. We fear other
nations, cultures, races, faiths or beliefs, states,
cities, counties, political groups, families, and, finally, individuals other than ourselves.

What is our choice? Censorship offers no answer,
since verdicts require judges, and evaluators may attack
a writer's finest instinct as well as the worst. Cen-

sors are mechanical. They ban four-letter words while
seven, eight, or nine-letter words often offer more
mental poison. All too often such judges even approve
a work that demeans humanity. Some "censors" are also
"critics." Frequently they abuse the privilege of telling us what to see and hear because, unfortunately, they
know so little about what they evaluate — the human condition. We read and consider their opinions because we
want to see a "hit" production.

The critic measures the work, but who measures the
critic? Whom can we wholly trust to tell us what is
"good" to see? Regarding the Black experience, we are
on particularly shaky ground, since no major Black critic now has the power to place a play, movie, book, or
other art work in the winner's circle. Major judgments
are made by White critics, who are not always unfair or
unenlightened, but the evaluators are theirs rather than
ours. We, of course, do not yet determine the success
or failure of White presentations; we usually are confined to criticizing one another. I see no remedy —
except for all of us to apply ourselves to a deeper examination and understanding of what we see, hear, and
read. One's own mind is the only one available for
full-time service.

Good theatre thrives on the complexities of human
experience and the passage of time. Even under restric-
tion, Black writers continue to emerge in greater num-
bers during this electronic age. Fully expressing deeply human feeling becomes more difficult when inflated
cost and popular opinion jeopardize mass media production. The writer faces many more executives who can say
yes or no to his work. Commerce makes deep inroads into
everyone's thinking. The situation is difficult, but
serious writers may still follow one rule. We must
write as we will, as we must; try to please ourselves
and be prepared to face and weather opposition, as well
as to accept approval. Some opposition will come from
those we try to please.

Many concerned people urge Black writers to improve
their characters' "image." A favorite portrait is the
Black person who has "accomplished" something under the
drastic conditions of a restricted life. But it is a
serious self-deception to think that culturally ignoring
those who are poor, lost, and/or rebellious will somehow

better our "image." If we will not see them, we must
also fail to see ourselves. The wrong is not in writing
about them but in failing to present them in depth, in
denying their humanity, in making them literary statis-
tics in social studies, and in using them in street
stories as humorous relief. Black writers cannot afford
to abuse or neglect the so-called ordinary characters
who represent a part of ourselves, the self twice de-
nied, first by racism and then by class indifference.

My great grandmother was a slave. I am not proud or
ashamed of that; it is only a fact. I believe a slave
is one who has lost a battle for the time being. I was
raised in Harlem by very poor people. My grandmother,
who went to the fifth grade in the Jim Crow school system of South Carolina, inspired me to observe what was
around me and to write about it without false pride or
shame, believing that there are some truths which are
very self-evident. I attempt to write about characters
without condescension, without making them into an image
which some may deem more useful, inspirational, profit-
able, or suitable. Listen for the poetry in common
prose, a sensitive experience.

Walt Whitman and Paul Laurence Dunbar approached
ordinary people with admiration and respect because
these poets realized that every human being has endless
possibilities. Sean O'Casey and Sholem Aleichem have
beautifully celebrated the poor Irish and the poor Jews,
as Paul Laurence Dunbar honored the poor Black slave
through love, understanding, and truth. The past, present, and future make for an untapped gold mine of literary material. I sincerely wish that writers, actors,
directors, and audiences will begin to view Black characters with the same human interest shown for Hamlet,
"the melancholy Dane."

RICHARD K. BARKSDALE

Langston Hughes: His Times and His Humanistic Techniques

In one of his critical essays, "Tradition and Individual Talent," T. S. Eliot suggested that there is a necessary creative tension between a given tradition and most writers who choose to write in that tradition. The tradition defines an approach and a set of guidelines that tend to restrict the creativity .of the individual writer, and the writer in reaction seeks to assert his independence and modify the tradition.[1] So tradition speaks to writer and writer speaks to tradition. At times, a writer affects a given tradition little or not at all. For instance, a nineteenth-century romantic poet like Philip Freneau did not change the tradition of romantic poetry at all. On the other hand, Algernon Swinburne, because of his literary and physical encounter with sadism and various kinds of eroticism, revolted against the tradition of Victorian neo-romanticism, and the tradition was never quite the same after Swinburne.

The case of Langston Hughes is not exactly comparable, but there is substantial evidence that by 1926, with the publication of his *Weary Blues,* he had broken with one or two rather well-established traditions in Afro-American literature. By no means was he alone in this act of literary insurrection; Claude McKay, Jean Toomer, and other poets of the 1920s stood with him. First, Hughes chose to modify the poetic tradition that decreed that whatever literature the Black man produced must not only protest racial conditions but promote racial integration. There was little or no place in such a literary tradition for the celebration of the Black

lifestyle for its own sake. With obviously innocuous
intent, Dunbar had attempted some celebration of the
Black lifestyle in the post-Reconstruction rural South,
but his pictures of happy pickaninnies and banjo-pluck-
ing, well-fed cabin Blacks did not square with the poverty and racial violence that seared that period. In
any event, by 1920 a poetry of strong social protest
which attempted to plead cultural equality with White
America had become a fixed tradition in Afro-American
literature. It was thought that Black America's writers
could knock on the door of racial segregation and suc-
cessfully plead for admission into a presumably racially
integrated society. Of course, admission would not be
gained unless these writers, painters, and sculptors
had all been properly schooled in Western techniques and
practices and thus fully qualified for acceptance. It
might be pointed out in this context that to effect this
end, even the so-called spirituals or sorrow-songs of
the slaves were Europeanized — songs whose weird and
sadly provocative melodies had had such a marked effect
on northern Whites when first heard on the Carolina Sea
Islands in 1862. In 1916, Harry T. Burleigh, the Black
organist at New York's ultra-fashionable St. George's
Episcopal Church, published his *Jubilee Songs of the
United States* with every spiritual arranged so that a
concert singer could sing it, "in the manner of an art
song." Thus, the Black man's art in song and story was
to be used primarily to promote racial acceptance and
ultimately achieve racial integration. And it was clear
that it had to be a Europeanized art.

Necessarily excluded from consideration in any such
arrangement was the vast amount of secular folk material
which had been created throughout the years of the Black
man's persecution and enslavement in America. For during slavery Black people had used song and story to
achieve many social and political goals. They had co-
vertly ridiculed "massa" and "missus" in song and story
and had overtly expressed their disdain and hatred for
the "niggah driber." And since slavery, they had sung
the blues on waterfront levees and in juke joints; they
had built railroads and sung about John Henry and other
laboring giants; they had been on chain gangs and as
prisoners had been leased out to cruel masters to cut
the tall cane on the Brazos to the tune of the slashing

whip and under a blazing sun which they called "Ole
Hannah." They had sung as they chopped cotton on tenant
farms and scrubbed and ironed clothes in the White
folks' kitchens. All of this orature, as some critics
have called it, was, in the opinion of certain twentieth-century monitors of Afro-American culture, to be
totally excluded from common view. Innocuous tidbits
might be acceptable, like James Weldon Johnson's "Since
You Went Away," which was one of the "croon songs" published in his 1916 volume _Fifty Years and Other Poems_.
But generally, the richly complex burden of secular folk
material — the songs and stories that came out of the
sweat, sorrow, and occasional joy of Black people of the
lower classes — might impede integration and hence was
to be expunged from the racial literary record.
The crystallization of a tradition which outlawed
Black folk literature and song inevitably fostered some
attitudes which adversely affected the jazz and blues
which were just beginning to be established in the early
1920s when Hughes first settled in New York City. For
the indictment of folk material resulted in the cultural
censure of the blues singing of Bessie and Clara Smith;
the jazz playing of Duke Ellington, Louis Armstrong, and
Fletcher Henderson; and the song-and-dance and vaudeville showmanship of Bill Robinson, Bert Williams, Eubie
Blake, and Noble Sissell. Ironically, one of the cultural monitors of the period, James Weldon Johnson, had
written that the cakewalk and ragtime were two of Black
America's principal contributions to American culture.
Johnson had been a music man himself at one time in his
career. But other strong-minded monitors of Black culture ignored Johnson and deemed that the dancing, singing, laughing, blues-singing, jazz-playing Black was too
uncomfortably close to a despised folk tradition to project a proper integrationist image. In retrospect, one
is forced to observe that in view of how deeply Black
jazz and music have influenced both twentieth-century
American and European lifestyles, this attempt to demean
the image of the Black entertainer and music man of the
early 1920s is indeed one of the great ironies in Afro-
American cultural history.
So Langston Hughes and other young poets of the early
years of the Harlem Renaissance had to confront a point
of view which had quickly crystallized into a binding

and restricting tradition. Hughes also developed a dis-
like for the tradition of racial exoticism which, largely promoted by White patrons, began to be an absorbing
concern of Black writers by the mid-1920s. Although his
resistance to racial exoticism eventually ruptured his
relationship with his patron, Mrs. R. Osgood Mason, his
fight against a tradition barring orature and the rich
folk material of the lower classes of Blacks became his
major struggle. The discussion to follow focuses not on
how he waged a successful fight to change that tradition, but on the humanistic techniques which he used in
his poetry to reflect and communicate the rich folk culture of Black people.

Before making any specific attempt to describe
Hughes's use of humanistic techniques in his folk poetry, one may make at least three generalizations about
his folk poetry. First, most of his folk poems have the
distinctive marks of orature. They contain many instances of naming and enumerating, considerable hyperbole
and understatement, and a strong infusion of street talk
rhyming. Also, there is a deceptive veil of artlessness
in most of the poems. Actually, there is much more art
and deliberate design than one immediately perceives.
I should point out in this context that Hughes prided
himself on being an impromptu and impressionistic writer
of poetry. His, he insisted, was not an artfully con-
structed poetry. But an analysis of some of his better
monologues and his poems on economic and social class
issues will reveal that much of his poetry was carefully
and artfully crafted. The third generalization is that
Hughes's folk poetry shares certain features found in
other types of folk literature. There are many instances of dramatic ellipsis and narrative compression.
Also, we find considerable rhythmic repetition and monosyllabic emphasis. And, of course, flooding all of his
poetry is that peculiar mixture of Hughesian irony and
humor — a very distinctive mark of his folk poetry.

The foregoing generalizations have a particular
relevancy when one studies some of Hughes's dramatic
monologues. In most instances, these are artfully
done; the idioms of Black folk speech and street talk
abound; and very often the final lines drip with irony
and calculated understatement. An example is "Lover's
Return":

> My old time daddy
> Came back home last night.
> His face was pale and
> His eyes didn't look just right.
> . . . .
> He says to me, "Mary, I'm
> Comin' home to you —
> So sick and lonesome
> I don't know what to do."[2]

First, there are two levels of monologue in this poem; the persona describes to the reader her elderly lover's return, and then, in lines which the poet italicizes, there is an interior monologue in which the persona talks to herself. These italicized lines clearly reveal the heightened anxiety and emotional tensions that haunt her:

> *Oh, men treats women*
> *Just like a pair o' shoes.*
> *You men treats women*
> *Like a pair o' shoes —*
> *You kicks 'em round and*
> *Does 'em like you choose.*

This interior monologue contains a repressed truth, and one can imagine the tremendous psychological pressure such a repressed truth has on the psyche of the persona. Moreover, these words in the interior monologue have a double-edged relevancy; they define the persona's particular dilemma and they also effectively generalize about a larger and more universal dilemma in the arena of sexual conflict. The full psychological impact of this monologue, however, is felt in the last stanza of the poem, where the conflict between outward compassion and inner condemnation is clearly delineated:

> I looked at my daddy —
> Lawd! and I wanted to cry.
> He looked so thin —
> Lawd! that I wanted to cry.
> But de devil told me:
> Damn a lover
> Come home to die!

Inevitably, as the result of the carefully controlled narrative compression commonly found in the well-crafted

dramatic monologue, many facts remain explicitly unstated. But Hughes calls upon the perceptive and imaginative reader to fill out the details of this miniature
but poignant drama. The persona, deserted by her lover
many years ago, is now forced by an obviously unfair
kind of social obligation to receive him once again.
Her code of faithfulness and her sense of social pro-
priety pull her in one direction. Her sense of fair
play and justice pulls her in another direction. In the
end, the harassed woman is torn between a deeply in-
stinctual desire to avoid pain and distress and a strong
sense of obligation to honor an elderly lover "come home
to die." Characteristically, Hughes defines the dilemma
and then leaves the resolution carefully unstated. By
so doing, he suggests that the vulnerable, dilemma-
ridden, anti-heroic persona truly counts in the larger
human equation.

Further examples of Hughes's humanistic techniques
can be found in certain of his blues poems and his dialogue and debate poems. In his gutsy reaction against
the tradition which censured the blues as offensive and
devoid of cultural import, Hughes wrote a lot of blues
poems. In fact, *Fine Clothes to the Jew* (1927), *Shakespeare in Harlem* (1942), and *One-Way Ticket* (1949) have
more than their fair share of such poems. Many are un-
complicated blues statements like:

> When hard luck overtakes you
> Nothin' for you to do.
> When hard luck overtakes you
> Nothin' for you to do.
> Gather up your fine clothes
> An' sell 'em to de Jew.[3]

or:

> I beats ma wife an'
> I beats ma side gal too.
> Beats ma wife an'
> Beats ma side gal too.
> Don't know why I do it but
> It keeps me from feelin' blue.[4]

In these poems there is a Hughesian blend of irony and
humor but no psychological complexity. One contains
some advice about how to handle hard luck with minimum

psychological damage; the second poem describes the
casual self-acceptance of a chronic woman-beater who apparently is unaware of the extent of his problem. But
in "In a Troubled Key" there is a difference. The blues
form is here, but the persona is emotionally insecure:

> Still I can't help lovin' you,
> Even though you do me wrong.
> Says I can't help lovin' you
> Though you do me wrong —
> But my love might turn into a knife
> Instead of to a song.[5]

The harassed persona is helplessly entwined in love, but
there is the possibility that instead of a song of love,
there will be knife-work in the night. Similarly, the
blues poem "Widow Woman" has an unexpectedly ironic ending. After promising to be ever-faithful to a recently
deceased "mighty lover" who had "ruled" her for "many
years," in the last two lines the persona suddenly becomes aware of the full import of the freedom that is
about to become hers. So the poem ends with the kind
of ironic juxtaposition Hughes loved. The outwardly
distraught widow stands sobbing by the open grave as she
watches the grave-diggers throw dirt in her husband's
face. But, inwardly, her heart soars joyfully at the
prospect of freedom: "...you never can tell when a /
Woman like me is free!"[6]

In addition to the humanizing techniques used by
Hughes in some of his dramatic monologues, the poet also
sometimes presented two personae in a dramatic dialogue
form of poetry. In one or two instances, the dialogue
broadens into a debate which the poet humanizes by carefully illuminating the two opposing points of view. For
instance, in "Sister," one of the poems in _Montage of a
Dream Deferred,_ a dialogue occurs between a mother and
her son about his sister's involvement with a married
man. The brother is embarrassed by his sister's behavior and asks: "Why don't she get a boy-friend / I can
understand — some decent man?"[7] The mother somewhat
surprisingly defends her daughter; actually her Marie
is the victim of the grim economic lot of the ghetto
dweller. She "runs around with trash" in order to get
"some cash." Thus a grim and dehumanizing economic determinism is in control of the lives of all three — the

mother, the son, and the daughter. The son, however,
still does not understand; he asks, "Don't decent folks
have dough?" The mother, out of the wisdom of a bitter
cynicism, immediately replies, "Unfortunately usually
no!" And she continues: "Did it ever occur to you, boy,
/ that a woman does the best she can?" To this the son
makes no reply, but a voice, probably the poet's, adds:
"So does a man." Hughes is saying that, like the distressed, fragmented, and fallible personae of most folk
poetry, human beings do the best that they can, and
their failures and defeats are actually the mark of
their humanity.

Another poetic dialogue, entitled "Mama and Daughter," has a slightly different thrust and meaning.
There is no polarizing conflict between the two personae, but obviously each reacts quite differently to
the same situation. The mother helps her daughter prepare to go "down the street" to see her "sugar sweet."
As they talk, the mother becomes increasingly agitated
because she remembers when she, too, went "down the
street" to see her "sugar sweet." But now the romantic
tinsel is gone forever from her life; her "sugar sweet"
married her, got her with child, and then, like so many
ghetto fathers, abandoned her to a life of unprotected
loneliness. So a dramatic contrast develops between the
naively hopeful daughter who is eager to join the young
man she can't get off her mind, and the disillusioned
mother who for different reasons can't get her errant
husband off her mind. When the mother expresses the
hope that her husband — "that wild young son-of-a-gun
rots in hell today," her daughter replies: *"Mama, Dad
couldn't be still young."* The anger of the mother's
final comment is the anger of all the abandoned women
of all of America's urban ghettos. And what she leaves
unsaid is more important than what she actually says:

> He *was* young yesterday.
> He *was* young when he —
> Turn around!
> So I can brush your back, I say![8]

Love and sex have tricked the mother and left her lonely
and full of bitter memories, but the "down-the-street"
ritual must be repeated for the daughter. Disappointment and disillusionment very probably await her later;

but to Hughes disappointment and disillusionment await
all lovers because these are, once again, the necessary
and essential marks of the human condition.

There are three other poems by Hughes which provide
interesting examples of his use of humanistic techniques. The first, "Blue Bayou," is a tersely wrought
dramatic monologue in which the persona describes the
circumstances leading to his death by lynching. In
essence, it is an age-old southern tale of an interracial love triangle that inevitably turns out badly for
the Black man. What is striking about the monologue is
the poet's use of the folk symbol of the "setting sun."
In some of the old blues standards, this image is a recurring motif with various overtones of meaning:

> In the evenin', in the evenin'
> When the settin' sun go down
> Ain't it lonesome, ain't it lonesome
> When your baby done left town.

or:

> Hurry sundown, hurry sundown
> See what tomorrow bring
> May bring rain
> May bring any old thing.

And at the beginning of "Blue Bayou," the "setting sun"
could be a symbol of "any old thing." The persona says:
"I went walkin' / By de Blue Bayou / And I saw de sun go
down."[9] Using the narrative compression and dramatic
ellipsis usually found in the folk ballad, the persona
then tells his story:

> I thought about old Greeley
> And I thought about Lou
> And I saw de sun go down.
>> White man
>> Makes me work all day
>> And I works too hard
>> For too little pay —
>> Then a White man
>> Takes my woman away.
> I'll kill old Greeley.

At this point, the persona's straight narration ends.
In the next stanza, sundown as a reddening symbol of

violent death is introduced, and the italicized choral
chant of the lynchers is heard:

> De Blue Bayou
> Turns red as fire.
> _Put the Black man_
> _On a rope_
> _And pull him higher!_

Then the persona returns to state with a rising crescen-
do of emotional stress: "I saw de sun go down."
  By the time the final stanza begins, "De Blue Bayou's
/ A pool of fire" and the persona utters his last words:

> And I saw de sun go down,
>   Down,
>   Down!
> Lawd, I saw de sun go down.

The emphasis in this last stanza is on the word "down,"
used four times in the four lines, and in lines two and
three "down, down!" are the only words used. And Hughes
arranges the monosyllabic words so that the second literally is placed "down" from the first. Thus concludes
this grim little tragedy of a triangular love affair
that ended in a murder and a lynching.
  Several additional critical observations may be made
about this poem. First, it is interesting to note how
Hughes manipulates the meaning of the setting sun. It
is done with great verbal economy and tremendous dramatic finesse. At the beginning, when the persona views
the setting sun, it is part of a beautiful Blue Bayou
setting. But the persona's mood is blue just like the
anonymous blues singer who shouts:

> In the evenin', in the evenin'
> When the settin' sun go down
> Ain't it lonesome, ain't it lonesome
> When your baby done left town.

Hughes's persona quickly and succinctly relates what has
happened to his baby, Lou. We do not know whether she
left voluntarily with old Greeley or had no choice. In
any event, as the sun is setting, the persona decides to
assert his manhood and kill old Greeley. A short time
after the deed is done, the lynchers catch him by the
Blue Bayou. Again the sun is setting, but now all na-

ture begins to reflect and mirror the victim's agony.
The bayou turns red with his blood; and then it becomes
a pool of fire mirroring the flames that begin to burn
his hanging, twisting body. Finally, the victim symbolically sees his own death as he repeats, "Lawd, I saw de
sun go down." It is through his poetic technique that
Hughes, the "artless" poet, conveys to the reader the
brutal and agonizing slowness of the persona's death.
Just as the setting sun in the American southland provides a scene of slow and lingering beauty as it sinks
down, down, down over the rim of the earth, so the death
of the victim is a slow and lingering agony as he sinks
down, down, down into the pit of death.

It should also be stressed that, although this poem
has a recurring blues motif in its use of the setting-
sun image, it has a finality hardly ever found in the
standard blues. In fact, all good blues reflect survival and recovery. In "Stormy Monday Blues," for instance, it takes Lou Rawls six days to get rid of his
blues; then, after the "ghost walks on Friday," on Saturday he "goes out to play" and on Sunday he goes "to
church to pray." In the real blues the persona is always waiting hopefully to see "what tomorrow brings."
But in Hughes's "The Blue Bayou," the persona has no
tomorrow. Had the poem described a tomorrow, the reader
would have seen a bayou flooded with the bright colors
of a beautiful sunrise; and, mirrored in the bayou's
sun-flecked waters, one would see the persona's body
slowly twisting in the early morning breeze. The stench
of burning flesh would be everywhere and no birds would
sing to greet the multi-colored dawn.

A discussion of Hughes's humanistic techniques in
poetry should include two additional poems: "Jitney,"
an experimental poem celebrating a highly particularized
mode of the Black lifestyle, and "Trumpet Player: 52nd
Street," which reflects the poet's consummate artistry
in one mode of genre description. Essentially, both are
folk poems. "Jitney" is an exuberant salute to the jitney cabs that used to wind up and down South Parkway in
Chicago and Jefferson Street in Nashville, Tennessee.
They have long been supplanted by better modes of transportation, but in the 1930s and 1940s the jitneys were
very much part of Black Chicago and Black Nashville.

In his poem, Hughes attempts to capture the unique-

ness of the experience of riding a jitney cab on two
round trips between Chicago's 31st and 63rd streets.
Like the cab, the poem snakes along; each stop — 31st,
35th, 47th — is a single line, thus providing the reader
with the sense of movement in space. Not only does the
form reflect the content in this poem; the form is the
content.

The great merit of the poem is not its experimental
form, however. "Jitney" is a microcosm of a moving,
surging, dynamic Black Chicago. Thus the poem celebrates not so much a mode of transportation unique to
Chicago's Black Southside; rather it celebrates the
Southside folk who ride jitneys and hustle up and down
South Parkway to go to church, to go to the market, to
go to night school, to go to nightclubs and stage shows
and movies. Or sometimes the time spent riding in a
jitney becomes a peaceful interlude in the hectic struggle to survive in a swiftly paced urban society — an
interlude to gossip or signify:

> Girl, ain't you heard?
> *No, Martha, I ain't heard.*
> I got a Chinese boy-friend
> Down on 43rd.
> 47th,
> 51st,
> 55th,
> 63rd,
> Martha's got a Japanese!
> Child, ain't you heard?[10]

As people come and go, facts and circumstances obviously change; but apparently the mood in a jitney cab is
one of warm, folksy friendliness — the kind Chicago's
Black residents remembered from their "down-home" days.
Indeed, the poem suggests that in a large metropolis
like Black Chicago, one refuge from the cold anonymity
of urban life is the jitney cab:

> 43rd,
> I quit Alexander!
> Honey, ain't you heard?
> 47th,
> 50th Place,
> 63rd,
> Alexander's quit Lucy!

> Baby, ain't you heard?
> . . . .
> If you want a good chicken
> You have to get there early
> And push and shove and grab!
> I'm going shopping now, child.

The pervasive mood of "Jitney," then, is one of racial
exuberance and vitality. As the cab moves up and down
South Parkway, the Southside folks who jump in and out
and are busy about their business have no time to talk
about deferred dreams. Obviously, Chicago's Black citizens had as many as Harlem's Black citizens; but the
jitney provided neither the time nor the place for in-
depth discussions of racial dilemmas. It is significant
that by the time Black urban America exploded into riot
and racial confrontation, the jitneys of Chicago's South
Parkway and Nashville's Jefferson Street had long since
disappeared from the urban scene.

Finally, "Trumpet Player: 52nd Street" reveals a fine
blending of the best of Hughes's humanistic techniques.
In the portrait of the musician we see both a particular
person and a folk symbol. For Hughes, who had started
writing about "long-headed jazzers" and weary blues-
playing pianists back in the 1920s, regarded the Black
musician as a folk symbol with deep roots in the racial
past. Thus in the poem's first stanza we greet the symbol, not the man. What the persona remembers, all Black
musicians have remembered throughout all of slavery's
troubled centuries:

> The Negro
> With the trumpet at his lips
> Has dark moons of weariness
> Beneath his eyes
> Where the smoldering memory
> Of slave ships
> Blazed to the crack of whips
> About his thighs.[11]

The instrument he is playing has no significance; it
could be a banjo, a drum, or just some bones manipulated
by agile Black fingers; the memory is the same. And the
memory makes the music different. Etched in pain, the
sound is better, the beat more impassioned, the melody
more evocative. And the music flows forth with greater

ease, as Dunbar's Malindy proved in "When Malindy
Sings." Actually these musicians have found the "spontaneous overflow of powerful emotions" that the youthful
Wordsworth was in search of and actually never found,
for too often in Western artistic expression, traditional structures intervene and negate spontaneous creativity.

The poem also has its fair share of Hughesian irony.
Where in ancient times man through his music sought the
moon and the beautiful, ever-surging sea, now matters
have changed:

> Desire
> That is longing for the moon
> Where the moonlight's but a spotlight
> In his eyes,
> Desire
> That is longing for the sea
> Where the sea's a bar-glass
> Sucker size.

So no fanciful escape from the hard facts of nightclub
life is permitted. We can and must remember the past
but we cannot escape the present, and through Hughes's
gentle reminder one stumbles on one of history's great
and o'erweening truths. If art does provide an escape
from the present, it is but a temporary escape. But the
memory of past pain and the awareness of the present's
difficulties and deferred dreams are themes that make
the *comédie humain* so truly comic.

Finally, as the poem draws to a close, the poet pre-
sents the trumpeter himself:

> The Negro
> With the trumpet at his lips
> Whose jacket
> Has a *fine* one-button roll,
> Does not know
> Upon what riff the music slips
> Its hypodermic needle
> To his soul.

The figure of the hypodermic needle penetrating the soul
of the music man suggests that the music provides only
temporary relief from the difficulties of the present:
jazz is a useful narcotic to allay the world's woes.

But the poetic image of the hypodermic needle also
suggests that jazz lovers can develop addictive personalities and become dependent on a little music that ex-
cludes the terror and woe of human existence. It is not
only good for the soul but absolutely necessary for the
psyche.

The final stanza of this extraordinarily well-made
poem repeats what was said at the beginning of the poem
about the historical role of the Black maker of music.

> But softly
> As the tunes come from his throat
> Trouble
> Mellows to a golden note.

The music anesthetizes both performer and listener
against remembered pain. In fact, the 52nd Street
trumpeter with his "patent-leathered" hair and his
jacket with "a *fine* one-button roll" disappears from
view and a folk music man of ancient origin reappears.
His role has long been to convert "trouble" into beautiful music. But Hughes humanizes the function of art
and music. In "Trumpet Player: 52nd Street" the poet
suggests that the Black man's music nullifies the pain
of the past and seals off the woe of the present. Ad-
mittedly, the poem, with its sophisticated imagery, is
probably not orature of the kind found in other poems
discussed above, but the Black music man described here-
in has long been a focal figure in producing the songs
and stories that Black people have orated and sung down
through the centuries.

There are many more instances of Hughes's use of
humanistic techniques throughout the full range of his
poetry. But this discussion has been limited to his
folk poetry — to his orature. It is now clear that
Hughes's devotion to this kind of poetry had two major
consequences: he broke the back of a tradition which
sought to exclude secular folk material from the canon
of Black literature. And, in his use of the language
of the Black lower classes, Hughes prepared the way for
the use and acceptance of the revolutionary Black street
poetry of the late 1960s.

[1]T. S. Eliot, "Tradition and Individual Talent," in *Modern Criticism* (New York: Sutton and Foster, 1963), p. 142.

[2]*Selected Poems* (New York: Knopf, 1959), p. 112.

[3]*Fine Clothes to the Jew* (New York: Knopf, 1927), p. 4.

[4]"Bad Man," in *Fine Clothes to the Jew,* p. 21.

[5]*Shakespeare in Harlem* (New York: Knopf, 1942), p. 49.

[6]*Selected Poems,* p. 139.

[7]*Montage of a Dream Deferred* (New York: Holt, 1951), p. 7.

[8]*One-Way Ticket* (New York: Knopf, 1949), pp. 31-32.

[9]Ibid., pp. 53-54.

[10]Ibid., pp. 131-33.

[11]*Selected Poems,* pp. 114-15.

MICHAEL S. HARPER

My Poetic Technique
and the Humanization
of the American Audience

The geographical division of the country into political districts and regions with complementary agricul-
tural and economic systems underlies much of Afro-
American poetic symbolism. That the star points
north is not important because of some abstract, or
mystical or religious conception, but because it
brought into conjunction Biblical references, concrete social conditions and the human will to survive
— including the fact that if you got safely across
certain socio-geographical boundaries you were in
freedom. Writers have made much of the North Star
but they forget that a hell of a lot of slaves were
running away to the West, 'going to the nation, going
to the territory,' because as Mark Twain knew, that
too was an area of Negro freedom. When people get to
telling stories based on their cooperate experience,
quite naturally such patterns turn up. Because as
significant scenes in which human will is asserted,
they help organize and focus narrative. They become
more poetic the further we are removed from the actual experience, and their symbolic force is extended
through repetition.[1]

I was fortunate enough to be born at home, delivered
by my grandfather, and so there was much lore attached
to my birth, much signifying. My parents weren't rich,
but they had a good record collection, and they prohibited me from playing any of their 78's, which was a

guarantee that I'd investigate in my own time, always
when they were out of the house. After dusting the
records, and making sure the needle was in place, the
records in the appropriate order, every item in place,
I'd forget not to hum the songs I'd heard, and would get
caught with a smile. I also had the habit of riding the
subway trains on what we called off-days, days when we
took off from school, all the Jewish holidays in particular. I'd been riding the subways since I was five, but
my parents didn't know it, and it took them three years
to catch me. On that fateful day I was illegally riding
after school, and passed my father as he went to work.
I knew he'd seen me, though he never let on, and I decided to get on the next train and continue riding.
At the next express stop I got off, intending to turn
around and go back home to the inevitable whipping when
I heard a tapping on a window of another train — it was
my grandmother. She waved faintly with a hint of a
smile. Music and trains! Coltrane. One learns most
by getting caught doing the things you love; it leaves
an impression.

I knew Bessie Smith and Billie Holiday from birth,
and I was a horn man: President Lester Young; Coleman
Superhawk Hawkins; Big Bad Ben Webster; Charles Chan
Parker, alias the Bird; John William Coltrane, alias the
Trane. There's a story that Trane was searching for a
particular tone on his horn. He had what we thought was
a perfect embouchure, but his teeth hurt constantly, so
he searched for the soft reed which would ease the pain.
After searching for a year, each session killing his
chops, he gave it up completely. There was no easy way
to get that sound — play through the pain to _a love
supreme_.

I wrote, secretly, in high school, buried in the back
of some English class for fear I'd be asked to stand and
recite a memorized poem of Donne, Shakespeare, or John
Keats. Luckily I tore up all these efforts, switched
to prose and short dramatic forms until I was almost
through college. I was working on the postal facing
table, the middle-class equivalent to the pool hall.
Almost everybody in sight had advanced degrees. It was
there I learned about Tolstoi and _So What_ Dostoevski,
as one of my partners used to call the Russian underground man. My partner had discovered Miles Davis.

When I went to the Writers Workshop at the University of
Iowa, I was the only blood in either fiction or poetry,
and I was enrolled in both. Several teachers asked me
was I going to be another James Baldwin — one of the
faculty members was so obsessed with Baldwin he knew
I'd known Mr. Baldwin — I had read Baldwin's novels and
essays, but hadn't met Baldwin personally. I began to
specialize in retorts to affronts. You met Isaac Singer? You been hunting with Hemingway? But this kind of
humor didn't go over very well. All the writers in the
workshop at the time were victims of the New Criticism,
the poets writing in rhyme and meter, the fiction writers reading James and Forster.

I hung out with the football players during the era
of Iowa's great dynasty. The best lineman on the team,
Al Hinton, would creep over to my garage apartment behind one of the few Black families in Iowa City, and ask
me if I knew anyone who could teach him to draw. We
were dancing to "Gypsy Woman" and playing tonk. I used
to stay in the library until closing time, 2 a.m., to
avoid the cold. My first and only poem on the worksheet
in the poetry class was a poem dedicated to Miles Davis,
"Alone," which I've since cut to three lines. It was my
bible. How would it be to solo with that great tradition of the big bands honking you on? Could one do it
in a poem? I'd taken my survey courses, studied my
Donne and Shakespeare, got hot at the Moor of Venice,
hotter at Prospero (me mad Caliban) and gone on to American literature without Frederick Douglass, Du Bois,
Johnson, or Toomer. Richard Wright I remember most
clearly because he was talked about in Brooklyn when I
was a kid. I read all his books in one weekend because
none of his books had ever been taken out of the school
library. I took offense at O'Neill's Brutus Jones (as
I'd despised Vachel Lindsay's "Congo" poem), and T. S.
Eliot's remarks on the ending of "All God's Chillun Got
Wings" (neither play large enough for the torso of Paul
Robeson), and searched for the cadence of street talk in
the inner ear of the great musicians. the great blues
singers.

This brings me to church. My mother was Episcopal;
my father Catholic; I was a Baptist because of the great
singing. Every Sunday I had to *hit the meter* (put money
in the collection box), hit the holy water, and take the

subway to 52nd Street to catch Bird play. One morning,
just after 9 a.m., Bird came out a side door, his sax in
a triply reinforced Macy's shopping bag: "Boy, how come
you not in church?" he asked, but I was quick, told him
I'd been and took up his horn case, the handles raggedly
stringed. He took us, three or four kids all under ten,
to the subway station; changed a quarter, gave us each
a nickel, told us not to sneak on the train going home,
and disappeared uptown.

I have images of musicians at their best and when
they were down and out; their playing never faltered —
the other musicians wouldn't tolerate anything less than
a journeyman job, a little extra inspiration. My people
were good storytellers. Some of my personal kin walked
north and west during the Civil War from North Carolina,
South Carolina, and Virginia, and one ancestor came from
Chatham — Ontario, Canada. I was surprised to find
their images in books, not Stowe's _Uncle Tom's Cabin_,
the play version differing greatly from the text of the
novel, but Douglass' 1845 narrative written by himself.
Douglass' rhetoric, the notion of having each slave
carry on his person an articulate pass, is my ticket
to freedom.

I have gotten letters from "friends" praising my
knowledge of history, but I learned a little terminology
from a zoology teacher in Los Angeles who had us count
somites in his worms. He told me I shouldn't study because I'd never get into medical school; I should pick
up a broom and forget the microscope. He, of course,
was being scrutinized for future reference. A new critic once wrote, "nigger your breed ain't metaphysical,"
and of course we're not. The poet, Sterling Brown,
whose record I heard in the library in San Francisco
fifteen years ago ("the strong men, keep a-comin' on /
the strong men, git stronger") coined an infamous retort
— "cracker your breed ain't exegetical."

I wrote about my "Grandfather" because he was a hero
in the highest sense, though he waited tables in white
clothes. He taught me to study Sugar Ray's left-hook
technique, to step inside someone's sense of time, of
theatre, of the stage and arena, and to floor show to
one's own tune. Ellison called it _antagonistic cooperation;_ Wright called it the switchblade of the movie-
screen. Language and rhetoric is essential power. Why

else were the slaves prohibited from reading, from
learning to pen their own sagas? All great art is finally testamental, and its technical brilliance never
shadows the content of the song. Deliver the melody,
make sure the harmony's correct, play as long as you
like, but play sweet, and don't forget the ladies.

A final note on the blues is that they always say *yes*
to life; meet life's terms but never accept them: "been
down so long that down don't worry me / road so rocky,
won't be rocky long." Johnny Hodges must have said this
to Duke on tour: "you run them verbs (the key of G),
I'll drive the thought (the rabbit on his own rainbow)."

I'll make a coda on the American audience, which is
vast potentially. "I wish you'd buy more books," said
Huck to Tom — meanwhile Jim was bringing his family to
freedom. The landscape of the poem is the contour of
the face reading the Declaration of Independence. How
many White Jeffersons are there in this country, anyway?
When I interviewed for my present duty at Brown University, all that slave trade money came back to haunt me
once again, a man yelled out from the genteel back of
the room that I was an impostor borrowing from musicians. Couldn't I do something about my accent? People
were embarrassed for him. He was quickly ushered out,
and the East Side returned to normal, good old Providence with its old money and the mafia flair. I remembered that Douglass had been run out of Providence to
New Bedford after an abolitionist meeting, and it's ru-
mored that John Brown (the fanatical one) came all the
way from Oberlin, Ohio, to meet the best gunsmith in
town, a Black infantryman from the Black Regiment of
Rhode Island.

"Straight, no Chaser," said the musician. He must
have meant the street corner and the library. With some
lies thrown in, this has been a riff in honor of my ancestors and a little stretching of the truth to make the
point. Here is one more lie to make the audience sweet.
When I was in South Africa in 1977 on an American Specialist Program, all by myself, I landed at Jan Smuts
airport in Johannesburg at about 2:30 a.m. I was carrying Sterling Brown's *Southern Road* and Robert Hayden's
Angle of Ascent and some of my own books, one with Coltrane's image on the cover. I was first addressed in
Afrikaans, but not being colored, I answered in Ameri-

can, "I'm from Brooklyn ... you ever heard of Jackie
Robinson?" It took me awhile to get through customs.
I was staying at the Holiday Inn right at the airport
so all I had to do was wait for the little van picking
up customers. I stood there for a few minutes, a few
Whites not far away. When the driver, a Black South
African, approached I got ready to board. I was first
in line. Telling me to wait, the driver held up his
hand to me, boarded all the White passengers, and drove
off. I stood there taking names so to speak. When the
driver returned, he apologized for not taking me in the
van with the other passengers. He wanted to know where
I came from and then he asked — "What language do you'
speak when the White people aren't around?" I said,
"English," and he said, "No, no." What language did I
speak when the White people weren't around? The second
time he asked I changed my response to "American."
"Brother," he inquired, "when Blacks are among themselves, don't they speak *jazz?*" I nodded, *right on,*
brother. Send more Afro-Americans from the states;
bring your record collections. The battle of the big
bands begins.

---

[1]Michael S. Harper and Robert B. Stepto, "Study and Experience: An Interview with Ralph Ellison," *Massachusetts Review*
18 (Autumn 1977): 435.

CHESTER J. FONTENOT, Jr.

Angelic Dance or Tug of War?
The Humanistic Implications
of Cultural Formalism

Humanism enjoys high prestige among modern intellectual movements; it is connected with a great number of philosophical ideas and has become vacuous. The term formalism, on the other hand, provokes its fair share of opponents among contemporary literary theorists. Formalism, for them, implies intellectual hypocrisy, esoteric aestheticism, scientific criticism, mundane pedagogical devices, and racism. To imply that the techniques of formalism apply to cultural criticism which has humanistic implications is to invite an angelic dance which inevitably degenerates into a tug of war.

To avoid such a battle — an arena stacked with anti-formalists convinced that I am trying to revive a dead horse — I should define humanism and the humanistic tradition. Once this definition is established I can attempt to purge formalism of its tendency to separate literature from culture, and to establish cultural formalism as a methodology for evaluating literature. Finally, I want to suggest the advantages of applying cultural formalism to Black American literature. This is a great task for a paper of this length, but I can begin to lay some groundwork. This effort should help literary critics interested in Black American literature to understand the importance of moving away from strict sociological approaches and to see Black writings first as creating cultural mores and values and second as reflecting social and ideological forces.

Distinguishing between humanism and the humanistic
tradition historically is unprofitable. Humanistic
seems to be the older of the two terms. Its origin lies
in the scholarship of the Italian humanists, who applied
the word *umanista* (a vernacular term later Latinized as
humanista) to students and professors of rhetoric. The
term humanism is of later origin. Used first by German
scholars of the early nineteenth century, it has come
to mean any philosophy which recognizes the value and
dignity of people, which makes them the measure of all
things, or which somehow takes as its theme human nature, its limits, or its interests. The first meaning
is historical. Humanism was the basis which Renaissance
thinkers used to reintegrate man into the world of nature and history and to interpret him in this perspective. The Renaissance scholars owed much to the Italian
humanists who sought a return to the Italian classical
tradition, to grammar, rhetoric, epistolography, and
oratory. The Italian humanists influenced elementary
and university education and established professorships
in these first two fields as well as in poetry. They
also made the humanities a well-defined area of scholarly disciplines (grammar, rhetoric, poetry, history,
moral philosophy), independent of other scholarly disciplines. The Renaissance humanists shared the Italian
scholars' interests in classical Latin and Greek, and
contributed philological and historical criticism. They
were concerned with moral problems and believed they
were living in an age of rebirth in learning and literature.[1]

One may quibble about the relationship of Italian and
Renaissance humanists and about the question of whether
humanism and Renaissance were intertwined movements
or separate intellectual currents. But if one accepts
the revival of classical scholarship as the underlying
characteristic of humanism, one can safely associate
the tradition with the rise of Italian humanism, which
reached its peak in the sixteenth century.

For purposes of this paper, the second meaning of
humanism is more fruitful. Literary study is distinguished by its concern for human beings, their interests, themes, and social organizations. In relation
to literature and literary criticism, humanism must deal
with the dialectic between human beings and their activ-

ities, between literary characters and their contextual situations. The humanistic impulse treats literature as the product of a human mind's attempting to come to terms with reality and as the result of a writer's reorganizing experience through language. And since language is the writer's means to envision the world, any critic's approach must give precedence to the creative power of language.

Many approaches to literature consider the constitutive power of the word. But formalism, when purged of its tendency to separate literature from society, can be moved from pure aestheticism ("art for art's sake") to cultural criticism. Such a proposal might, at first glance, seem a fruitless academic exercise and a demonstration of an irresolvable contradiction in method. Yet, by considering formalism within its own historical period, one can modify many of the charges raised against the formalists and find formalism culturally appropriate for the study of Black American literature.

Originally formalism was a derogatory term which the Marxists applied to a group of Russian scholars in the early twentieth century. In America the movement began around 1923, with its initiators Allen Tate, John Crowe Ransom, R. P. Blackmur, Kenneth Burke, and Yvor Winters; its later advocates were Cleanth Brooks, Robert Penn Warren, William K. Wimsatt, T. S. Eliot, and I. A. Richards. These critics were reacting against four main movements in American criticism. Rene Wellek says: "There was, first, a type of aesthetic impressionistic criticism, a type of 'appreciation,' ultimately derived from Pater and Remy de Gourmont, prevalent in the first decade of this century. James G. Huneker may stand here as the representative figure. There was, second, the Humanist movement, of which Irving Babbitt and Paul Elmer More were the acknowledged leaders.... Then there was, third, the group of critics who attacked the 'genteel' tradition, the American business civilization, the 'bourgeoisie,' and propagated the naturalistic novel, Dreiser's in particular.... Finally there were the Marxists who flourished during the Great Depression in the early thirties."[2]

Though one might quarrel with the tendency to lump Ransom, Tate, Blackmur, _et al._, together as a group (since they disagreed on fundamental assumptions about

literature), they stand as a coterie of emerging in-
tellectuals who were opposed to the four main currents
in American criticism during the early decades of the
twentieth century. Together they rejected the mystical
criticism practiced by the impressionists. Tate, Blackmur, Burke, and Winters in particular were critical of
the neo-Humanists and denounced H. L. Mencken and Van
Wyck Brooks, especially when Brooks found that he had
little use for Modernism. Nearly all of the New Critics
summarily rejected Marxism, except for Kenneth Burke,
who passed through a Marxist phase en route to his work
with symbolic form as language.

The New Critics rejected academic English literary
scholarship, characterized by philological and historical methods. These two methods were the basis of humanism in its historical sense. The New Critics rejected
"scientific" approaches to literary scholarship, as well
as psychological, economic, and sociological approaches.
Their major purpose, rather, was to develop a kind of
criticism which would anticipate historical judgment, or
what one commonly calls "the test of time." But rejecting historical scholarship is not the same as abandoning
the historicity of literature. The New Critics realized
the need for historical perspectives in evaluating hu-
mane letters and were actively involved in evaluating
the history of English poetry. Rather than advocating
"art for art's sake," they separated aesthetic experience from utilitarian concerns. They maintained that
the aesthetic experience necessitates separating the
work of art from the phenomenal world and comprehending
the work in its totality, seeing its unity and coherence
by its own internal laws. They minimized external standards, such as history, sociology, and politics. This
distinction among aesthetic beauty, scientific truth,
morality, and practical utility had its foundations in
Kant's seminal work *Critique of Judgment* (1790). The
idea that a work of art has internal cohesion, however,
dates as far back as Aristotle and came to English and
American critics through Coleridge.

Yet the New Critics did not see literature as totally separate from reality. Brooks's famous statement
against the "heresy of paraphrase" was an attempt, not
to set poetry apart from reality, but to insist that a
poem cannot be reduced merely to scientific truth, to

a verifiable statement about reality. The proposed fic-
tional nature of art does not mean that art can have no
relation to reality, either directly or indirectly, and
it certainly does not mean that the poet is entrapped in
a "prison house of language," where language becomes a
separate reality. Many of the New Critics upheld a mod-
ified version of mimesis or imitation. But for the New
Critics poetry constituted reality, not merely a reflec-
tion of it.

Unlike scholars preoccupied with genres, the New
Critics actually paid little attention to poetic form,
as one would expect from the term "formalism." From
time to time they spoke of poetic meter and stanzaic
forms, but they were more concerned with rejecting the
distinction between form and content. The New Critics
differed markedly from the Russian formalists in that
the former were primarily concerned with the meaning of
a work of art, but saw the meaning as the verbal inter-
plays within an organization which distinguishes itself
from other kinds of communication. The crucial distinction between "formalism" as a method and the New Critical method is that the former attempted to separate art
from social reality while the latter saw art as both
reflecting and creating reality. The main objections
to the New Critics' brand of formalism came from the
Chicago Aristotelians, who emphasized plot, character,
and genre, and from the archetypal critics who saw myth
as a system of metaphors or symbols carrying universal
meanings. The New Critics valued myth as one concern,
but the myth critics tended to exclude other qualities
of art while stressing myth, which became so vacuous as
to include almost any image, theme, or story.

The Geneva School and its American followers, the
critics of consciousness, joined the Chicago Aristotelians and the myth critics in rejecting New Criticism.
But the demise of the New Criticism was finally the result of the general movement against aesthetics, the
rejection of aesthetic contemplation as an independent
state of mind. Rene Wellek says that "the New Criticism
has become a victim of the general attack on literature
and art, of the destruction of literary texts, of the
new anarchy which allows a complete liberty of interpretation, and even of a self-confessed nihilism."[3]

The New Cultural Formalists, a label which implies

contradictory methodologies, attempt not to revive the
brand of formalism practiced by either the Russian formalists or the New Critics, but to reveal the human
content of art by investigating its formal principles.
This does not mean that cultural formalists embrace "art
for art's sake." Art has a functional purpose in a culture, but its purpose is not external to its nature.
The purpose of a work of art is first to maintain unity
and coherence as an edifice which has its own integrity,
and second to serve utilitarian purposes.

Cultural formalists differ from either the Russian
formalists or the New Critics in that they do not think
that art has an existential object to which it refers,
but believe that art does "mean something." Cultural
formalists attempt to find a position which will trap
them in neither a theory of imitation nor one of pure
formalism. Perhaps the best example of a critic who
could be called a cultural formalist is Eliseo Vivas.
In an essay, "The Object of the Poem,"[4] Vivas takes up
a question which is fundamental to literary theory: In
what sense can we say that the poem has an object other
than itself? Vivas works through this problem and develops the concepts of "subsistence," "insistence," and
"existence." These terms refer to the various stages
in which a poem operates and creates culture, and they
chart the process from the moment of the poem's creation
to its existence as an object of culture. Vivas uses
the term culture to refer to "the interrelated constel-
lation of activities of a social group, insofar as these
activities, the social institutions through which they
are carried on, and the physical instrumentalities that
make them possible, embody values that enable the group
to maintain itself as a purposive, distinctly human society; the meanings are the social structures as value
carriers; the culture is the total pattern of values
carried in the meanings."[5]

These meanings, though an integral part of the culture, are not fully realized by the members of the culture; these meanings "subsist" in the culture. The poet
discovers these meanings by fixing them in language and
in the work of art; these meanings are artistic form.
The artist's gift, in other words, "consists in discov-
ering the not-yet-discovered subsistent values and meanings that make up his poem's object in the creative act

which is the revelation of that object in and through
the language to his own and to his reader's minds."[6]
When these meanings are brought to the realization of
both the poet and his audience, they have "insistence."
This act of creation, which Vivas calls "discovery," is
important because it is only through formalizing the
meanings in language that these values and meanings are
realized. Prior to this process, the cultural values
are "disembodied," without meaning or form, and thus do
not exist. Vivas says, "The poem is a linguistic thing
which reveals symbolically in and through its medium
meanings and values which have subsistent status in being and which are discovered by the poet in the act of
creation. Note that the word 'discover' is intended
literally, for the meanings and values embodied in the
poem do not exist prior to their embodiment. They are
found by the poet in the creative act in a realm beyond
existence where they subsist."[7]

Once abstractions are made from the poem, the "insistence" is thinned into "existence," in which form the
meanings operate in the culture. The participants in
the culture "get the impression that its [the poem's]
object imitates meanings and values with which they have
been more or less well acquainted all along."[8] But this
is not so. The poem brings the meanings and values of
the culture to its participants' attention. The poem
performs a normative function; the participants espouse
the values and meanings which the poem reveals.

Richard Wright's *Native Son* is an excellent example
of the three stages discussed above. Before publication
of *Native Son,* the various Black responses to communism,
to Blacks' inability to become full participants in
American life and culture, and to the oppression of
Black people in cities had not been fully expressed in
Black writings. Of course, one can point out that Black
American literature begins with personal statements
against oppression (i.e., slave narratives). But the
harsh conditions in which Black people lived combined
with their constantly being faced with choosing between
competing ideologies had not been addressed in a novel
until Wright published *Native Son*. The meanings and
values of Black culture with respect to urban oppression
and warring ideologies were, in Vivas's terms, subsistent, disembodied. The cultural power of Wright's novel

centers in his ability to discover Black culture's response to these problems and to work these meanings and
values out in language. By externalizing Black cultural
values through language, Wright pioneered a unique artistic form — the Black protest novel — which had been
attempted previously by only a limited number of Black
authors.

The publication of *Native Son* brought the Black cultural mores and values to the attention of Black Americans. At this stage, these values had insistence; they
were given meaning and form through linguistic shaping.
The utilitarian uses Black literary critics and social
activists assigned to *Native Son* comprise the cultural
mores' existent state. The critical response to *Native
Son* championed the novel as an expression of cultural
meanings of which Black Americans had been cognizant.
This critical posture led critics to evaluate *Native Son*
sociologically, to see the novel as discursive. These
literary and social critics failed to consider the process of linguistic shaping and the effect the poetic
object — once its meanings and values "exist" in the
culture — has on its audience.

Cultural formalists attempt to take into account the
way language shapes and creates cultural meanings and
the dialectic between the poetic object and the cultural
participants. Vivas's analysis is enlightening, but
perhaps a bit oversimplified. One can distinguish between different processes of "creative discovery." On
the one hand, one can speak of an artist who has an experience and writes about it. The artist uses his experience as material for his vision, which he attempts
to work out in his writings. The vision is inchoately
formed; the act of writing is an attempt to give shape
and coherence to this vision so that it will become concrete and communicable to others. One could speak, on
the other hand, of an artist who is concerned, not with
having an experience and writing about it, but with de-
veloping a vision through a critique of the past. The
artist is still working toward an ideal, a previous notion which is incomplete and partially blurred; but
unlike his counterpart, the process of writing is the
forming of the vision. The vision gains more and more
externalization as the artist reworks his own position
and uses his experience as a basis for his critique.

The central difference here is that the first process works toward a vision which is already present but not completely formed; the second process develops a vision through a dialectical process. In the latter, one knows what the vision lacks but one does not know what it has.

Cultural formalists are involved in distinguishing between artifacts and social contracts. There is a correlation between the two kinds of experience. Both involve vivid imaginations; both use language as a medium to build their system of thought; both suggest that they can literally change people's perceptions of reality and people's response to these perceptions. The imaginations of the poet and the social critic appear to oppose each other because the former is primarily concerned with having an experience or with using someone else's experience as poetic material, a means to an end. For the poet this experience need not be empirical, nor must he remember the experience exactly as it occurred. He is primarily interested in subordinating his experiences to the demands of his form, and this allows him to produce a poem. The poet thinks of his vision as something being made in the act of writing, not as something his art "copies."

In contrast, the social critic also sees himself as working to make something, but the difference is that he does not necessarily see what he is making as a slant on reality which is incomplete and in need of reworking. He is likely to think of his creation as an "objective" representation of reality, and of his work as effectively having exhausted all possibilities. The end product for the social critic is not to rework his vision to produce a finished and complete poem but to rework society or to create a new society. Instead of concerning himself with generating an experience through vision, the social critic focuses his attention on shaping the presentation of the future through a critique of past experience, a dialectical process. This distinction still requires him to order his critique in language and to "construct" a past to criticize. The social critic sees himself as a materialist or realist, while the poet sees himself as a critical idealist.

Both intend their vision to provide one with the opportunity to transform present reality, but the activity by which they conceive of such a process is different.

The poet sees his structure as providing the means to transform present reality through the reworking of past social and poetic traditions. By giving concreteness and form to previous visions — which to the poet are all incomplete — he can awaken an audience who can participate in those visions. The social critic, however, not only sees past social traditions as incomplete, but also insists that they are completely wrong. His work is not directed at reworking past traditions; it is focused on destroying all previous traditions, making way for a new social order which will correct the wrongs the previous society perpetuated. The poet makes his experience in a symbolic form, thus creating an obvious fiction; the social critic casts his past experience in a symbolic form with great caution. This is because the poet is aware that his structure is the creation of a human psyche and that it has a "fictive" element in it, making it incomplete. The poem he produces is an effort to externalize this vision, and each revision is an attempt to give more and more form, concreteness, and externalization to the vision. In a sense, one can say that each revision is an attempt to "find" his vision through linguistic shaping. The social critic, on the other hand, by insisting that all previous traditions are clearly wrong and that he has "discovered" the "objective" nature of social conditions, finally implies that his expression of what he sees as the past is a copy of the past. For the social critic, his structure is not necessarily a fiction but an objective statement about the world. His structure is complete.

The most important difference between the poet and the social critic is the nature of their beliefs. In *Opus Posthumous,* Wallace Stevens speaks of this distinction as follows: "The final belief is to believe in a fiction, which you know to be a fiction, there being nothing else. The exquisite truth is to know that it is a fiction and that you believe in it willingly."[9]

Here it is possible to distinguish between two types of social critics. One insists on the objectivity of his structure and on the correctness of his insights. This type of social critic sees himself as an analyst and not as a creator. He is, of course, a creator insofar as the things he discovers in his analysis are unique to his structure. The other creates with the

intent of awakening an audience to participation. This
type of social thinker is consciously aware of the fictive nature of his structure, and he is balanced between
the analytical methods of the pure scientist and the
creative activity of the mythmaker and artist. This
difference is crucial in that the former is more likely
to create a structure which will allow a reader to exhaust its possibilities by extracting discursive statements from it. The reader is likely to find that the
discursive statements he abstracts from the structure
effectively exhaust the number of possibilities in the
fiction and, in fact, include more possibilities than
the construct itself. Once this happens, society is
likely to discard the structure because the structure
is of little use to anyone. The latter type of social
critic may be able to create a system which will withstand attempts to reduce it in this manner. By main-
taining distance from his own creation, by constantly
reworking his own position to keep it "open," and by
struggling with language to keep it from "hardening,"
this second kind of social critic may create a structure
which can prevent externalization and closure.

In *Invisible Man,* Ralph Ellison treats the problem
incurred by a social critic who insists that his fiction
exhausts all possibilities, and that this structure is
closed and demands a single interpretation. The nameless hero of this novel (identified only by an invisible
"I") confronts a character named Ras the Exhorter, a
fictionalized version of Marcus Garvey, the leader of
the back-to-Africa movement in the early twentieth century. Ras has created a system which he thinks will
alleviate the plight of Black people by returning them
to Africa. He insists that all other Black organizations which seek to combat oppression through other
means (i.e., separatism, integration, and so on) are deceitful and are little more than agents for the "white
establishment." Ras the Exhorter finally changes his
name to Ras the Destroyer, which symbolizes the change
his system has undergone — he has moved from an ideolo-
gist and social activist and visionary to a dogmatist;
he finally turns his structure into a closed system and
seeks the destruction of those who refuse to conform to
his demands. At one point in the story, the hero confronts Ras at a community rally where Ras is the speak-

er. Ras says: "Look, look, Black ladies and gentlemahn!
There goes the representative of the Brotherhood. Does
Ras see correctly? Is that gentlemahn trying to pass us
unnoticed? Ask _him_ about it. What are you people waiting for, sir? What are you doing about our black youth
shot down beca'se of your deceitful organization?"[10]
The Brotherhood represents the Communist Party, of which
the hero becomes a part. Both the Brotherhood and Ras
represent Black organizations which attempt to approach
and solve the problem of oppression in different ways,
and both insist upon the correctness of their own viewpoints. Ras implies here that the Brotherhood is responsible for the death of a Black youth because of its
accommodationist tactics. If it had not been for the
Brotherhood's trying to come to terms with the White establishment, Ras accuses, the boy would not have been
killed. Ras would have been allowed to confront the
police violently and to try to neutralize their potential danger. These accusations, combined with the char-
ismatic charm Ras displays, finally create a following,
and Ras convinces the people that the only way to end
oppression is to wage war against the system. This, he
insists, is the single method which will combat both the
establishment and the Black organizations which support
it. Clothed in fit costume, Ras "had him a big black
hoss and a fur cap and some kind of old lion skin or
something over his shoulders and he was raising hell.
Goddam if he wasn't a _sight,_ riding up and down on this
ole hoss, you know, one of the kind that pulls vegetable
wagons, and he got him a cowboy saddle and some big
spurs."[11] Ras finally succeeds in awakening the revolutionary potential in the inhabitants of Harlem, and
armed with spear and shield he leads them to combat.

The police enter Harlem with the intent to break up
the riot, at which point they are confronted by Ras, now
turned into the Destroyer. When he sees the police,

> He lets out a roar like a lion and rears way back and
> starts shooting spurs into that hoss's ass fast as
> nickels falling in the subway at going-home time —
> and gaawd-dam! that's when you ought to seen him!...
> Here he comes bookety-bookety with that spear stuck
> out in front of him and that shield on his arm,
> charging, man. And he's yelling something in African
> or West Indian or something and he's got his head

down low like he knew about that shit too, man; riding like Earl Sande in the fifth at Jamaica. That
ole black hoss let out a whinny and got *his* head down
— I don't know *where* he got *that* sonofabitch — but,
gentlemens, I swear! When he felt that steel in his
high behind he came on like Man o' War going to get
his ashes hauled! Before the cops knowed what hit
'em Ras is right in the middle of 'em and one cop
grabbed for that spear, and old Ras swung 'round and
bust him across the head and the cop goes down and
his hoss rears up, and old Ras rears his and tries
to spear him another cop, and the other hosses is
plunging around and ole Ras tries to spear him still
another cop, only he's too close and the hoss is
pooting and snorting and pissing and shitting, and
they swings around and the cop is swinging his pistol
and every time he swings old Ras throws up his shield
with one arm and chops at him with the spear with the
other....[12]

But his violent attack is not confined only to the
police or to the members of the "system" — the nameless
hero again confronts Ras, only to find that the Destroyer has gone mad:

Someone called, "Look!" and Ras bent down from the
horse, saw me and flung, of all things, a spear, and
I fell forward at the movement of his arm, catching
myself upon my hands as a tumbler would, and heard
the shock of it piercing one of the hanging dummies.
I stood, my brief case coming with me.
　"Betrayer!" Ras shouted.[13]

Ras continues to threaten the hero, to refuse to
hear anything the hero has to say in defense of himself.
Finally, in a desperate attempt to free himself of the
demands Ras continues to thrust on him, the hero "let
fly the spear and it was as though for a moment I had
surrendered my life and begun to live again, watching
it catch him as he turned his head to shout, ripping
through both cheeks, and saw the surprised pause of the
crowd as Ras wrestled with the spear that locked his
jaws."[14]
Here Ras's structure crumbles, and his followers finally realize that the mindless violence Ras has perpe-
trated on Harlem has been useless. The symbolic act of

throwing the "spear that locked his jaws" represents the
realization that the system is closed, that its possibilities have been exhausted, and that it cannot bring
social change.

In some ways, the plight of the poet and the social
thinker resembles the classroom instructor's dilemma.
One of the instructor's main concerns is to develop a
method of teaching, a structure, a way of looking at education which is responsible, and in which he has some
confidence. Once the instructor enters the classroom,
however, he must be careful not to present his system as
dogma (closed), even though he is constantly pressured
by students who seek to reduce the instructor's creation
to verifiable facts about the external world. Only
through a constant reevaluation of his pedagogical position can the instructor succeed in promoting free inquiry. Through research and scholarly investigation,
he is trying to rebuild his creation, to reconstruct it
in the ruins created by incessant attempts to abstract
"facts" from the structure. Once the instructor allows
his mode of analysis to succumb to the temptation of
what Blake called the "stubborn structure of the language," he is no longer capable of stimulating intellectual inquiry in the classroom. Instead, he becomes
a "preacher," a dogmatist inside his own system, an
espouser of his own rhetoric.

Closed and open, as used here, refer to the nature of
a symbolic structure. The distinction concerns whether
one can judge the creation in terms of its truth or
falseness or whether one can judge it in terms of the
number of discursive statements it can generate. Here
it is useful to distinguish among four possibilities in
regard to symbolic structures: 1) an open fiction; 2) a
closed structure which insists on a single interpretation or a limited number of "levels of meaning" (what
in the romantic period began to be called "allegory");
3) a fiction which its author intends to close but which
remains open; and 4) an open fiction which the reader
has distorted into a closed system. This last type of
fictive system is really a variety of type one.

The first possibility appears to be the most powerful
because it forces the reader to see that any opinion he
may abstract from the structure is partial and that at
best it only gives one a fragment of the potential myth.

This type of fiction resists reduction to truth or
falsehood, and it is quite clear to the reader that he
cannot subject it to this test. This is because (to use
Vivas's terms) at the stage of insistence, the structure
emits a number of discursive statements which reveal the
meanings and values of the culture. When the reader abstracts these statements from the fiction, or the existent state, the "insistent" nature of the structure
forces one to see that it has many possibilities.

The second category also clearly shows its nature to
the reader, but here the nature is quite different. A
closed system forces one to verify it as true or false.
Its claim of having contained within it all possibilities leads one to see it as a single interpretation
which must, by definition, be judged either correct or
incorrect. If the interpretation is judged incorrect,
the structure is discarded as artificial or misleading.
If it is judged correct, the structure becomes a belief.

The third alternative is the result of the author who
intended to write a closed assertion but whose structure
finally turned out to be open. The confusion about this
type of fiction is grounded in its creator. The fourth
possibility is grounded in the reader, and is perhaps
the most problematic of all. The reader simply refuses
to see the infinite possibilities in the structure and
insists on reducing the entire myth to a single statement which can be proven either true or false. The
potential power of the myth is effectively harnessed.
Any statement the reader abstracts from it can only be
a partial interpretation. This is a common problem for
the classroom instructor, whose students often want to
close systems or find the "answer" to a puzzle.

The fourth type of symbolic structure is important to
the study of Black American literature, for too often
critics have sought to reduce a poem, a novel, or a play
to a single statement which could be tested against the
Black American experience to determine the literary
object's cultural and social value. Critics of Black
American literature have insisted that Black creative
writings are no different from discursive essays, and so
must serve directly the interests of oppressed people,
especially Black Americans. These critics have applied
the sociological approach (which one critic has called
sociologizing about literature) *ad nauseum* to Black

American literature, and have insisted that these writings must first be judged in terms of their utility.

The various approaches which stem from such a vantage point on literature fail to distinguish between artistic objects and discursive essays, to evaluate the purpose of each as an integral unit in a culture, and to distinguish between literature capable of generating profound insights about Black American culture and writings which are merely assertions of a particular sociocultural milieu. The tendency to exclude aesthetic judgments about literature as "elitist" and "irrelevant" has meant that the sociological or positivistic urge (to use a pejorative term) has swayed the opinions of many critics, publishers, and students with regard to Black American literature.

Black writers use their own and other Blacks' experiences as the basis for any critiques. But the Black American experience is not a monolith; it has varied sides and shapes. Each writer attempts to discover creatively the meanings and values which are applicable and pertinent to particular communities. He creates a symbolic structure which both creates and reflects the Black experience.

Some critics of Black American literature claim that paying close attention to the symbolic structure of the writings is accepting a mode of analysis which is foreign to the works. These scholars, students, and readers fail to see the potential harm they do to Black American literature, for they have insisted that it is not literature but political rhetoric. For Black American literature, formalism in its most convoluted form has contributed to cultural and artistic strangulation, and criticism has been forced to redirect its system of humanistic inquiry. Cultural formalism encourages its user to alleviate the tension between formalism and the humanistic impulse in Black American literature, between pure formalism and mimesis. Cultural formalism permits him to criticize Black American literature from a base where the ontological status of the poetic object lies in its identity as both an autonomous creation and a manifestation of human culture.

[1]For a more detailed account of the history of humanism, see the following: Paul Edwards, ed., *The Encyclopedia of Philosophy* (New York: Macmillan and Free Press, 1967), 4:70-72; Philip E. Wiener, ed., *Dictionary of the History of Ideas* (New York: Scribner, 1973), 2:514-23; 4:129-35.

[2]I am indebted to Rene Wellek's insightful essay, "The New Criticism: Pro and Contra," *Critical Inquiry* 4 (Summer 1978): 612.

[3]Ibid., p. 623.

[4]Eliseo Vivas, "The Object of the Poem," in *Creation and Discovery* (New York: Noonday Press, 1955, reprinted in Hazard Adams, ed., *Critical Theory since Plato* (New York: Harcourt, Brace, 1971), pp. 1069-77.

[5]Ibid., p. 1073.

[6]Ibid., p. 1074.

[7]Ibid.

[8]Ibid.

[9]Wallace Stevens, *Opus Posthumous* (New York: Knopf, 1957), p. 163.

[10]Ralph Ellison, *Invisible Man* (New York: New American Li-

[11]Ibid., p. 486.

[12]Ibid., pp. 487-88.

[13]Ibid., p. 482.

[14]Ibid., p. 484.

TRUDIER HARRIS

Three Black Women Writers and Humanism: A Folk Perspective

Christianity is usually assumed to be one of the major influences on Blacks in the United States; it is considered the force that shapes behavior and establishes guidelines for conduct. While this may be true on a large scale, it is not universally true, either in history or in literature which portrays the Black experience. While Black writers frequently have shown that Christianity influences the behavior of their characters, they have recognized other influences as well. Humanism may often be a more satisfying philosophy than Christianity. While a code of ethics such as humanism may have Christianity as its basis, it may move outside the realm of church beliefs and derive from some other source. One source is Black folk tradition, where many characters find the basis for interaction with other characters. Because folklore and folk culture continue to inform and inspire the creation of much Black American literature, we must return to this source for guides to the humanistic conceptions on which many Black writers base their creations.

Along with writers and critics, folklore scholars have repeatedly pointed out that their subject is the base for Black American literature. The history of Blacks in the United States is so compact that the pattern from folklore to conscious art is easily traceable. In a country where, as late as 1823, there were laws which prohibited Blacks from learning to read and write, it is no wonder the folk or oral culture had to retain the values of the group. These values remained perhaps

in a more vivid form than those in other cultures which
were freer to make the transition to literature. Ralph
Ellison maintains that folklore contains the specific
forms of Black humanity, as well as what is "worth pre-
serving or abandoning" in the background of Black Americans. Folklore, he asserts, "offers the first drawings
of any group's character. It preserves mainly those
situations which have repeated themselves again and
again in the history of any given group. It describes
those rites, manners, customs, and so forth, which insure the good life, or destroy it; and it describes
those boundaries of feeling, thought and action which
that particular group has found to be the limitation of
the human condition. It projects this wisdom in symbols
which express the group's will to survive; it embodies
those values by which the group lives and dies."[1] The
folk culture binds those conscious creators of Black
literature to their roots and contains the basic metaphors for their experiences in America.

Those experiences are still informed by the socio-
historical pains of slavery, which Ellison points out
were essential to the shaping of Black life. "Negro
folklore," he writes, "evolving within a larger culture
which regarded it as inferior, was an especially cour-
ageous expression. It announced the Negro's willingness
to trust his own experience, his own sensibilities as to
the definition of reality, rather than allow his masters
to define these crucial matters for him."[2] Ellison's
comment is crucial because a common misconception about
folklore and folk culture is not its assertiveness but
its passivity. Slaves dealt with their lot as best they
could — so the misconception goes — but mainly they sang
and laughed and were happy and prayed to go to heaven.
Even if they glimpsed the reality of their situation in
a song such as "We bake the bread, they give us the
crust," they nevertheless gave themselves up to waiting
for that great watermelon pie in the sky. How could the
lore they created and passed on embody complaint and desire for freedom if they accepted the tenets of Christianity? And those Black folk were (another assumption
goes) childlike, innocent, and credulous in their Christian beliefs. They trusted in God to guide them and ex-
plained their experiences as the Lord's will. The Christian God stood beside them; they needed nothing more.

I maintain that religion — here Christianity specifically — did and does not embody the values many Black folk wanted to preserve. When the choice is between Christian resignation or faith and humanistic action or reason, literary characters, like their folk counterparts, often reject Christianity in favor of a more exacting and humanistic idealism. They reject the easy way out in favor of more challenging solutions. Sarah E. Wright's Mariah Upshur, Alice Walker's Grange Copeland, and Paule Marshall's Merle Kinbona are all steeped in Christianity and Black folk culture. Yet the goals they set for themselves, their aspirations for peace, freedom, and happiness, go beyond Christianity. Here a code of ethics has the folk culture as its basis, although it transcends the limitations of folklore as well.

This code determines models for love and sacrifices that are willingly made for others. It suggests the mode by which one defines self and the refusal to allow that self to be violated. It determines the line that is drawn between humanness and animality, and it provides a base for the choices the characters make concerning living and dying. They believe in self-determination, and they gladly accept the responsibility for this belief. Instead of an externally imposed God, they look to their secular heritages in folk tradition and to their inner selves for guidance in their actions.

The choices they make between the secular and the Christian reflect patterns in their folk cultures. Newly arrived from Africa and accustomed to visible gods, slaves found it strange that White men worshipped gods they could not see. The slave was encouraged to give up his "heathen" ways, but even when he professed belief in the Christian God, his need for a tangibly supernatural force was not satisfied. He turned to the hoodoo doctor and his little red flannel bags and doll-like images. He prayed that God would bring his loved one back or that his master would not beat him so frequently, but he didn't trust prayer alone. He would take his meager barter of a chicken or a few ears of corn and go to ole Aunt Sarah or ole Uncle Ed down the road from the plantation and ask for a spell to bring the loved one back, or a piece of high john the conqueror root to carry in his pocket to keep the master

from whipping him. Christian and folk beliefs existed
side by side, more in harmony than in conflict. Christian symbols and images were appropriated to secular
concerns. Many references compare the Jews in bondage
in Egypt to Blacks in slavery in the South. Anonymous
creators of folk songs and spirituals appropriated religious imagery to the plight of the slave. References
to Canada acquired the additional meaning of Canaan,
the Promised Land. The spiritual "Steal Away," referred
just as easily to stealing away *from* the plantation as
stealing away *to* Jesus. Moses, the deliverer, became
Harriet Tubman, conductor for the Underground Railroad.
In the novel by folklorist Zora Neale Hurston entitled
Moses, Man of the Mountain (1939), Moses becomes more
than an emissary empowered by God; he becomes the most
powerful conjure man around.

In making Moses more glamorous from the folk point of
view, Hurston vividly employed the tradition of Chris-
tian/folk coexistence; thereby illustrating the historical need Blacks felt for something other than Christianity to guide their behavior. To the slave, Christianity
was seldom a strong enough force in itself. It had to
be bolstered and, if necessary, rejected when something
more was needed. Christian morality could be pushed
into the background in favor of the amorality of Brer
Rabbit, the trickster, or of John, the slave who used
his wits to appropriate more food for his family or to
get his freedom from Old Marster. The folk characters
were applauded, if not emulated. Christian values
failed as guides for what was right. Folk creations
allowed for a broader glimpse into the workings of human
nature. Usually they encouraged interactions on levels
of mutual humanity and respect instead of the master/
slave relationship which Christianity supported.

These interactions sustained a humanistic approach to
life. When the slave was violated in some way, he could
adopt the amorality of Brer Rabbit; he could turn to the
bosom of Jesus; or he could move to something beyond
either of these. He could use his folk emphasis on
humanity to define his relationships with others. He
could establish for himself a code of ethics based not
on God but on human values. Following the tradition of
their folk ancestors, characters in the works to be considered here by Sarah Wright, Alice Walker, and Paule

Marshall manage to do just that. They pattern their
lives according to values Peter Faulkner recognizes as
humanism in "its modern sense of an ethic which places
human happiness as its central concern and is skeptical
about the supernatural and transcendental.... The emphasis is on mutual human responsibility.... The spirit
of humanism is flexible and undogmatic, refusing to
sacrifice human happiness to any rigid orthodoxy....
Humanism is a philosophical position, not a matter of
casual good-will, and its basis is the belief in human
responsibility and human potentiality."[3]

Mariah Upshur, the protagonist in Sarah E. Wright's
This Child's Gonna Live,[4] epitomizes conscious creation
in literature based on folk tradition, but she is also
a character who grows into a humanistic response to
life. Mariah represents folk culture before urban in-
dustrialization. She lives on the eastern shore of
Maryland where her community is rural, isolated, unedu-
cated, small-town-gossipy, one-church, and strictly
moral. With other inhabitants, she believes in weather
signs, dreams, and superstitions. She thinks one can
read nature by knowing its signs and predict the future
from symbols and images that come to mind during sleep.
This Child's Gonna Live is the story of Mariah's
struggle to retain some semblance of humanity in a world
that would dehumanize her, to act individualistically
and humanistically in a world of petty jealousies and
hypocritical "Christians." She wants her unborn child
to come into the world healthy and sane and to stay that
way. This reasonable wish takes on added dimensions
when we know that Mariah, at twenty-three, is pregnant
for the fifth time, and that she is married to Jacob, a
"going-nowhere" man whose strange conceptions of pride,
manhood, and familial identity will not allow his wife
to accept welfare or the charity of a hospital delivery.
It is equally important that her three living children
are tuberculoid, wormy, undernourished, and improperly
clothed. When the novel opens, Mariah must go out and
dig potatoes all day long for the mere subsistence of
the family. Finally, it is significant that Cleveland's
Field, the local cemetery in which several generations
of Upshurs are buried, looms like a prominent character
throughout the story. The threat of death from signs,

weather, and the physical presence of the graveyard
enhances Mariah's determination that her unborn child
should live. The specific determination, however, becomes generalized into Mariah's hope that all her children will live and grow, that they will get educations
despite the school's financial trouble, and that they
will escape from Tangierneck, the Neck. "My children
ain't no fowl and brute," Mariah says. "I wants my
children to live. They human beings just like anybody
else" (p.7).

Against the forces that would deny her individuality,
Mariah must evolve a code of behavior that will save her
emotionally, offer her spiritual security, and direct
her interactions with others. In order to accomplish
these goals, she must reevaluate and ultimately reject
Christianity. She could easily lose herself in religion, for her situation is a classic struggle, and yet
she ultimately refuses the balm. When the novel opens,
Mariah's voice implies a middle-aged, work-worn woman
nearly overcome by poverty and work. The voice is frustrated, demanding, hopeful, and frustrated again. Her
words and actions blend folk wisdom with a desire for
religious stoicism. The curious mixture of the Christian and the folk characterizes Mariah throughout the
story. On close examination, however, her Christianity
becomes sounding brass and tinkling cymbal. She has the
words but not the substance of Christian conviction.
She calls on God by habit, crying out for signs that she
questions and negates before they are revealed to her.
God is as much a part of her upbringing as is Cleveland's Field or the Gut, where her husband works. Yet
the substance of faith is absent. There is no doubt of
Mariah's sincerity and her desire for help when she
cries out, but she does not resign herself to passive
acceptance of things unseen. She desires a faster response to her requests than God's mysterious ways. Soon
after the novel opens Mariah awakens thinking her unborn
child may be dead. "My child's all right, ain't it,
Lord?" she pleads. "Spare the child, Lord, and I prom-
ise you, if I use every last bit of strength I got, we
getting out of this place" (pp.12,13). But Mariah takes
no comfort from her prayer. It is only when the child
kicks viciously in her womb that her worry is eased.
Whatever faith she has must be reinforced by the ration-

al, tangible element of the baby's kicking. The supernatural alone does not insure comfort and resignation.

Mariah has reduced Jesus and God to the role of
conversational buddies. She diminishes the distance
between the Almighty, the divine, and the supplicant,
the human. This reduction takes her further away from
Christianity as the guide for living. Jesus becomes a
familiar companion who is addressed without reverence
and who perhaps takes the place of Mariah's nonexistent
friends. She uses such phrases as "Jesus, you must
think I'm crazy," "Excuse me, Jesus," and "Jesus, you
know I thanks you." Mariah is also blasphemous. At one
point she envisions herself executing a kind of legendary revenge on the White man who oversees the potato
fields (pp.3-5). She imagines herself a kind of folk
hero in the bad nigger vein, daring to do what nobody
else would. She uses profanity, plays the dozens, and
calls on God, all in the same breath. She ultimately
compares herself to Jesus running the money-changers
from the temple; she will in turn reorder the Black situation with Whites. While these acts might condemn Mariah from a Christian point of view, they simultaneously
intensify her determination for a betterment of her relationships with other human beings.

Tangible experience makes Mariah lean toward the human and the natural rather than the supernatural. She
has also learned very vividly that an unbridgeable chasm
divides Christian theory and Christian acts. The strict
moral code of the community, based on the Bible and the
church, suits individual purposes more than God and
Christian values. Several years before the novel opens,
as a result of a camp meeting incident where one of her
pregnant young neighbors died, Mariah was forced to con-
fess her illegitimate first pregnancy to the church
members. Called a liar when she claimed Jacob as the
father of her child, she was whipped unmercifully by her
mother from the church to her house. Until Jacob returned months later and married her, she remained in a
tiny room. She discovered that Christianity equalled
White morality. The keepers of morality in the church
were only concerned that Mariah and young girls like her
would make public spectacles of themselves and embarrass
Tangierneck in front of Whites.

When leaving the church, Mariah initially rejects the

religious domination of her life. Church attendance,
however, does not necessarily predetermine belief. By
her refusal to be reincorporated into the bosom of the
church, she reinforces the earlier physical rejection.
And her blasphemy sets her further apart. Perceiving
the double standards of morality of the representatives
of Christianity in her community, she finally seeks another code of ethics. She bases her actions on what she
senses intuitively. Reasoning about the best possible
alternatives for herself and her children, she turns to
the values of her folk heritage.

Mariah joins her folk ancestors in considering freedom essential to human happiness and in distinguishing
between humanness and animality. Slaves sang of their
desire for escape from the toil of slavery and the
abuses of their bodies. The North Star became a vivid
symbol of that desire, which Frederick Douglass captured
in his famous newspaper. For the generation of Blacks
who succeeded slavery, the North became a mythic place
where all Black troubles would be over if only the price
of a one-way ticket could be scraped together. Mariah
perhaps does not believe in the myth of the North as
wholly as her ancestors, but it is still a symbol of
escape for her. She reasons that its unseen sights must
offer a favorable contrast to her present situation.
When she envisions leaving the Neck, she imagines telling anyone who should ask where she is going: "I'm on
my way to the North. Going to the city where me and my
children can act in some kind of dignified way" (p.5).
The city here is Baltimore. Although all three of
Jacob's brothers eventually are brought home dead or
come home from there to die, the deaths do not dimin-
ish Mariah's vision that somewhere there must be something better. There must be a place where pregnant
women don't have to dig potatoes all day, where "going-
nowhere" men will perhaps be inspired, and where gifted
children can develop into the poets they obviously have
the talent to become. Mariah emphasizes education for
her children more than anything else. "Get something
in your head, boy," she tells her son Skeeter (p.24).
Education will be a liberating force, Mariah believes,
and she holds to that belief when Jacob is unsupportive
and when the women of the community scorn her desire for
better things.

We see Mariah's humanism in her other relationships,
too. She refuses to drown Miss Bannie, the White woman
who controls all the land Jacob's father and grandfather
owned at one time and who continually exacts rents the
poor inhabitants cannot afford. Mariah finds Miss
Bannie on a path one night after she has been beaten by
Pop Percy, Jacob's father. Mariah decides to drown the
"lynch-bait woman," but even at the water's edge she
knows she cannot kill. She needs reasons to justify
this change of mind. Her baby kicks violently, and her
body is doubled over with hiccoughs. She imagines her
water bag has broken. All of this happens as she alter-
nately talks to Jesus and tries to follow through with
murder. Her physical discomforts are merely excuses to
get out of what she knows she cannot do. Even when she
says "White people ain't no good, nohow" (p.136), she
cannot bring herself to destroy another human being.
Her commitment is to life, and the life in her womb resists murder.

Ethically Mariah's final growth is her refusal to
commit suicide, although she contemplates it on two
occasions. After her many trials and tribulations, it
would be easy to fall into the final rest of death. It
would be easy, after the community scorn of her, her
husband's sexual rejection, and her best friend's be-
trayal, to welcome the escape. But she does not. She
goes to the rough waters of the Gut and wades in up to
her knees before stopping (pp.271-72). Dedicated to
life and freedom, she cannot condone the action. She
chooses to continue being responsible for her own children and those she has adopted. She turns from the
water and passes Jacob on the way home. In answer to
his frantic questions about whether she intended to
drown herself, her only response is, "I forgot to put
the dough to bake in the oven so you and the children
could have some nice hot bread for your dinner" (p.272).

Mariah grows from the need for external and supernatural reassurances to a philosophical strength. Her
progression is sometimes explicit but more often impli-
cit. Whereas Mariah is able to act out her humanistic
growth more than to verbalize it, the protagonist in
Alice Walker's *The Third Life of Grange Copeland*[5] combines action and philosophical expression. Steeped in

folk tradition and religion, he is dehumanized more
greatly, and before he can understand humanism, he must
recover his own humanity.

The novel is the story of a man who must first discover that he is indeed a man and then make choices in
his relationships with other human beings. Caught in
a sharecropping system in Georgia in the 1920s, Grange
Copeland deteriorates into debt and self-degradation
and lacks any apparent means of escape. He is married
to a beautiful woman who cannot return to him the self-
respect the Whites have taken away. His son Brownfield
illustrates Grange's inability to control his life and,
indeed, to become a father. In an effort to salvage
something of the manhood slipping away from him, Grange
takes to making Saturday night visits to another woman.
His equating manhood with sexual prowess is one of the
first things he has to alter before he can grow into a
true understanding of humanity.

Grange does attend church, but he has little faith.
Even at the beginning of the novel, he has progressed
further than Mariah has in rejecting Christianity, but
he has not yet found another system of ethics. As an
animal, he goes through the motions of living. His
subhumanity is reinforced in the early chapters of the
novel by his appearing through Brownfield's eyes. In
narrative technique Grange is distanced from the reader,
just as he is distanced from Margaret and Brownfield in
his relationships with them. Their lives are a cycle
of existence, predictable and hopeless. Each day brings
endless work, sighs, and gloominess. On Thursday nights
the dehumanization is particularly apparent: Grange
"stalked the house from room to room and pulled himself
up and swung from the rafters of the porch" (p.20).
Grange dresses and visits his other woman on Saturday
nights, returning home late and threatening to kill Margaret and Brownfield. He "would roll out the door and
into the yard, crying like a child in big wrenching sobs
and rubbing his whole head in the dirt. He would lie
there until Sunday morning, when the chickens pecked
around him, and the dog sniffed at him and neither his
wife nor Brownfield went near him. Brownfield played
instead on the other side of the house. Steady on his
feet but still ashen by noon, Grange would make his way
across the pasture and through the woods, headlong, like

a blind man, to the Baptist church, where his voice
above all the others was raised in song and prayer"
(pp.20-21). Grange goes to church by habit, not by conviction. But participation in church services brings no
relief. Later, he and Margaret "would begin a supper
quarrel which launched them into another week just about
like the one before" (p.21).

Unlike Mariah, Grange gives up on himself. He loses
his hope, his manhood, and his humanity. He accepts the
classification that Shipley, the White man who owns the
farm where he works, has given him. He becomes a mere
brute of labor, a mule to be driven, a tireless ox. He
becomes as unfeeling as a lump of clay. In wallowing in
his own troubles, he forgets his wife and son.

Falsely believing that geography can determine ethics, he rejects his first life and goes north to that
mythic land of opportunity and freedom. He leaves behind a wife who poisons herself and her illegitimate
second child. Brownfield, the son, will follow the path
of irresponsibility. Grange abandons the slavery of
sharecropping and the escapist mentality of religion.
He cannot, however, transcend his psychological condition. It has resulted from years of accepting other
people's definitions of who he is. Ironically, he follows his ancestors to New York, not to find liberation
but to become even more dehumanized and enslaved. He
trades the morality of the church for the amorality of
Brer Rabbit, the trickster and con artist. He becomes
the active animal, as opposed to the passive one in the
sharecropping life. He holds no respect for other human
beings or for their property. Ready to rob, steal, and
assault if necessary to survive, he becomes a monster
lurking in dark shadows. From the caged animal on the
plantation in Georgia, he progresses to the wild animal
on the prowl in New York.

Still Grange does not grow into complete awareness of
his humanity. He resists being considered a "thing,"
but cannot recover himself and regain his lost humanity.
He must reach the depths of dehumanization before rising
from the mire. Bottom, for him, is deciding to let a
young pregnant White woman drown. The incident occurs
one night in Central Park when Grange tries to return
some money the woman has dropped nonchalantly after being abandoned by her lover. Grange could take the seven

hundred dollars and disappear, but something in the
woman's appearance draws him toward her: "in a matter
of seconds, his feet turned themselves in the direction
of the young woman.... he could think of no matterable
difference between them. Misery leveled all beings, he
reasoned, going after her" (pp.158-59).

Grange's decision to follow the young woman is the
first genuinely unselfish human response he has had
since leaving Georgia. He is drawn to the woman's suffering and to their human kinship. She refuses his
help, however, and pushes him back into the category
of "thing." She insults him and tosses the money into
the pond when he offers it to her. When the insults
cause Grange to fight back, the woman falls into the
pond in her effort to escape from him. Here Grange
understands that human beings do have a responsibility
toward each other. "Now he realized that to save and
preserve life was an instinct, no matter whose life you
were trying to save." He acts upon that awareness:

> He stretched out his arm and nearly touched her.
> She reached up and out with a small white hand that
> grabbed his hand but let go when she felt it was
> *his* hand. Grange drew back his dirty brown hand and
> looked at it. The woman struggled to climb the bank
> against the ice, but the ice snagged her clothes,
> and she stuck in the deep sucking mud near the steep
> shore. When she had given him back his hand and he
> had looked at it thoughtfully, he turned away, gath-
> ering the scattered money in a hurry. Finally she
> sank. She called him "nigger" with her last dis-
> gusted breath. [p.161]

This is Grange's first opportunity to regain his lost
manhood, to come back into the human race. He fails because he still cannot transcend other people's evalua-
tions of him. The woman, like Shipley, reduces him to
something inhuman, and he *accepts* that evaluation. No
matter how other people think and feel toward him, he
cannot allow that to define his conception of himself.
He must, as Ellison said, trust his own sense of reality. Even if he had forcibly saved the woman, that
would have restored his humanity, no matter what she
thought. He would have accepted his responsibility
toward another human being.

Yet the incident is not all failure. Although Grange cannot accept responsibility for the woman's life, he does accept responsibility for her death. The acceptance begins his liberation from "thing" to man and starts him toward a more secure set of values. He had gone north looking for a physical freedom, only to discover that freedom is a state of mind. And to be free is not necessarily to be guiltless. In his second life Grange accumulates experiences and begins the self-growth that will culminate in his return to Georgia and his third life.

What Grange has learned in the North provides him with the strength to face what he finds upon his return. Back in Georgia, he discovers that Brownfield is perhaps even more immoral and animalistic than Grange ever was. Brownfield has let sharecropping dehumanize him to the point of beating his wife and brutalizing his children. He has none of Grange's desire to escape, and he wallows in his own dehumanization. Recognizing and accepting his role in the creation of this monster, Grange tries to atone for his own actions by helping Brownfield's family. Brownfield, however, is unregenerate. When he kills his wife, Grange takes in Ruth, Brownfield's youngest daughter, and through his relationship with Ruth, Grange reaches his full human potential. We see his commitment to human happiness and his desire for peace and freedom.

It is significant that Grange's increased involvement in human relationships is still not motivated by any externally imposed set of values. He determines what is right for him as a thinking individual. He chooses to take Ruth, although no court urges her adoption. He chooses to work for her happiness because he views himself as her one human source of comfort, and this element of choice again emphasizes a humanistic orientation. Grange's return and his actions do not signal a religious conversion; rather, they signal a continued growth in responsibility for human situations.

Grange maintains his independence of church doctrines in spite of going to church, reading the Bible, and encouraging Ruth to read it. From the church's viewpoint, he is a sinner who drinks, gambles, and dislikes White folks. He laughs openly in church at men who pray fervently when they know they have beaten their wives on

Saturday night. His philosophy is governed by his own
experiences, which have taught him a pattern for living
and for dying. This becomes clearer when Brownfield,
released from jail, comes demanding custody of Ruth.
He does not want her, for he has never loved his children. He merely wants Grange "to sweat" and experience
fear in payment for his early injuries against him.
Brownfield and Grange have suffered similar dehumanization by Whites, but Brownfield never grows beyond the
externally imposed definitions which limit his humanity.
He remains the monster Grange has progressed beyond.
Grange's experiences have taught him that to remain voluntarily in the role of beast, as Brownfield does, makes
the White man divine. It suggests that the White man
creates and destroys, that he has ultimate power.
"'Cause when they got you thinking that they're to blame
for *every*thing they have you thinking they's some kind
of gods! You can't do nothing wrong without them being
behind it" (pp.214-15). Grange fully understands the
consequences of blaming everything on Whites. It is
this understanding that makes his progression in the
third life complete:

> The crackers could make me run away from my wife, but
> where was the *man* in me that let me sneak off, never
> telling her nothing about where I was going, never
> telling her I forgave her, never telling her how
> wrong I was myself?... And with you [Ruth's] pa...
> the white folks could have forced him to live in
> shacks; they might have even forced him to beat his
> wife and children like they was dogs, so he could
> keep on feeling something less than shit. But where
> was the *man* in him that let Brownfield *kill* his wife?
> What cracker pulled the trigger? And if a cracker
> did cause him to kill his wife, Brownfield should
> have turned the gun on himself, for he wasn't no man.
> He *let* the cracker hold the gun, because he was too
> weak to distinguish that cracker's will from his!
> The same was true of me. We both of us jumped our
> responsibility, and without facing up to at least
> *some* of his wrong a man loses his muscle. [pp.215-
> 16]

Here is a morality that goes not only beyond Christianity but beyond racial considerations. The individual

must be responsible to his humanity. Whites may be powerful; they may be able to put Blacks in subservient positions. But Grange maintains to Brownfield, *"you got to hold tight a place in you where they can't come"* (p.216).

Grange teaches Ruth the lesson. If all conception of humanity is lost toward Whites, it may also be lost toward Blacks. The result would be a numbness that could separate an individual from all human intercourse. When Ruth comments that numbness is probably better than hate, Grange responds: "The trouble with numbness...is that it spreads to all your organs, mainly the heart. Pretty soon after I don't hear the white folks crying for help I don't hear the black" (p.218). He impresses upon her the necessity of fighting if Whites try to abuse her, and then cautions: "But I don't want you to fight 'em until you gits completely fagged so that you turns into a black cracker yourself! For then they bondage over you is complete" (p.219). Ruth must re- frain from becoming the animal her father is and from identifying with the power of the Whites, who would also reduce her to an animal.

Grange's philosophy and his life are brought to a test when Brownfield takes Grange and Ruth to court in a custody suit. The judge, who has had illicit dealings with Brownfield, is sympathetic toward him and decides against Grange and Ruth. Understanding all the reasons for the judge's actions, Grange shoots his own son dead in the courtroom. Grange and Ruth return to the farm, not in an attempt to escape but because Grange has cho- sen his dying ground. Still he protects Ruth. Although he has taught her to shoot, he sends her into the house unarmed, as he draws the policemen to a cabin he and Ruth have shared. In Grange's mind, Ruth is still inno- cent, and she still has a chance for happiness. She has survived her mother's death. She will survive his, he believes, if his lessons have taken hold. He had sur- vived many degradations, "But to survive *whole* was what he wanted for Ruth" (p.222).

Earlier Grange had said, "if one kills he must not shun death in his turn" (p.162). He is true to that be- lief. "A man what'd do what I just did," he tells Ruth, "don't deserve to live. When you do something like that you give up your claim" (p.254). Finally, Grange ac-

cepts responsibility for life and death. Brownfield was
the monster he created and Brownfield was the monster he
decided to destroy. Grange, too, will in turn be de-
stroyed. His recognition of this two-way responsibility
completes his philosophical position. As he sits by the
cabin, dying from a gunshot wound, he still refuses to
recognize any values, any pattern for his life other
than what his own humanity defines. In reflex, he opens
his mouth "in a determined attempt to pray.... He could
not pray, therefore he did not." To do so would deny
his entire life of independent action and free will.
He cries out to himself because he needs "the sound of
a human voice" and he rocks himself "in his own arms to
a final sleep" (p.255). He has lived and died by his
choices.

Merle Kinbona, a forty-year-old West Indian woman, a
central character in Paule Marshall's *The Chosen Place,
The Timeless People,*[6] shares with Grange Copeland experiences of degradation and denial of humanity. She also
experiences a psychological stasis which she must overcome if she is to find a system of values of her own.
When the novel opens, Merle is back on Bourne Island
after a disastrous sojourn in England. While in London
she became the "pet" of a wealthy Englishwoman who de-
manded sexual favors and entertainment in return for the
financial support Merle received. After years of ex-
ploitation and dehumanization, Merle breaks from the
woman and marries an African by whom she has a daughter.
When the vindictive Englishwoman reveals all, the African takes the child and leaves. Merle has a nervous
breakdown, which leaves her subdued and indifferent to
her personal improvement. She also experiences recurring cataleptic states if she becomes unduly upset. Her
head is "set out," and the friends who care for her wait
patiently for her return. Marshall succeeds in making
Merle a source of strength in spite of lapses. Merle's
active involvement in the folk culture of Bournehills
will provide her with the guidelines for values she must
use to find herself.
    Bournehills has a folk culture in the traditional
sense. It is the most isolated and rural part of Bourne
Island, outside the progressive district of New Bristol
and separated from the rest of the island. The hill

that marks the beginning of Bournehills symbolizes the
culture and "backwardsness" with which other Bourne
Islanders associate it.   In Bournehills progress breeds
skepticism.   Inhabitants ignore or sabotage the grand
schemes of anthropologists to modernize and enhance the
quality of life.   These attempts are always doomed to
fail.   The past is a continuing part of the present, not
only spiritually but physically.   Here the seventeenth
century merges with the twentieth; here the family's
dead watch over unattended children (there are also many
references to obeah and duppies); here, it is said, the
crashing waves are the sea's mourning for the nine mil-
lion Blacks who died in the Middle Passage.   Mirrors
must be draped so the family's dead will not look at
themselves, and the eyes of the dead must be closed
quickly before they look upon someone else, so hastening
his death.   In the days of British subjugation, the legendary Cuffee Ned led a slave revolt here, like that of
the Maroons in Jamaica.   And though his head was severed
from his body, his spirit, like Marie Leveau's, lives on
in his descendants.

The Cuffee Ned story contains the elements that Merle
will adopt as her humanism.   Peace, freedom, and the refusal to allow the self to be violated are the qualities
that Cuffee, the legendary folk hero, instilled in his
people, the traditional values which Merle inherits.
When she can fully accept Cuffee's guidelines for living, she can truly regain her psychological health.
Because the Cuffee Ned legend defines Bournehills, and
because Merle is so much a part of Bournehills, to understand Merle it is necessary to understand the legend.
Cuffee Ned, a seer and shaman, led a revolt of slaves
against the White landowners.   Pyre Hill, the site of
one landowner's house, was burned, and the fire continued (legend has it) for five years.   Cuffee and his
followers defeated part of a British regiment and became
a nation apart in Bournehills.   For three years they
had a model community.   Dependent upon themselves, they
worked together.   When the British regiment was reinforced, Cuffee and his followers were eventually defeated, but not before holding off the troops for six
months.   Cuffee died happy because "he had seen his life
and deeds as pointing the way to what must be" (p.288).

"What must be" is self-determination which will lead

in turn to pride and a sense of community. Self-
determination necessarily has self-definition as its
basis. What Merle needs exists in the folk tradition.
How the local community responds to that tradition provides another measure for fusing humanism with the
choice about life. The people value Cuffee's upheaval
above all else; local rum shop frequenters argue end-
lessly about the number of months Cuffee held the British at bay. Mr. Douglin, an aged Bournehills man, has
one function in life — every day he ceaselessly and un-
tiringly cuts the grass on the spot on Westminster Low
Road where Cuffee's severed head hung for weeks "as an
example." Even Merle violates custom and is fired for
teaching New Bristol students about Cuffee. And, fusing
past and present more vividly, a pageant reenacting
Cuffee Ned's revolt is the Bournehills people's yearly
contribution to Carnival. They exclude themselves from
consideration for prizes by refusing to change their
pageant. They willingly suffer the scorn of more progressive Bourne Islanders by refusing to forget that old
stuff. Under Cuffee, the members of the pageant sing,
"a man had not lived for himself alone, but for his
neighbor also. 'If we had lived selfish, we couldn't
have lived at all.'... They had trusted one another, had
set aside their differences and stood as one against
their enemies. *They had been a People!"* (p.287).

Cuffee Ned's revolt provides an internal definition
for the people of Bournehills. When the Shipleys of the
island wanted to reduce them to brutes, they defined
their own reality by humanistic self-determination and
passed that on to the Bournehills people of Merle's generation. Still, the outside influence is strong in
Bourne Island, not only in the Black petty bourgeoisie
(decidedly British imitations) and the White absentee-
owners of nearly all the sugar cane land and their resi-
dent flunkies, but also in the presence of the Anglican
church. Old Black women sit like zombies in the candle-
lit Anglican church intoning hymns. The scene is
strangely incongruous, for the women obviously feel
the presence of duppies more than that of Jesus Christ.
They go through only the motions of worship. Perhaps
in the habitual manner of Grange Copeland, Merle often
joins the group. But the substance of faith is absent.

Merle discovers that more is needed for living than

dependence on Christianity. Supernatural forces and
stylized patterns of behavior cannot satisfactorily
determine community; flexibility is needed. On two
occasions Merle briefly discusses religion with Saul
Amron, an anthropologist working in Bournehills. She
laughingly maintains that God doesn't want her and Saul
responds that the Devil probably doesn't either. "The
church and the rumshop!" Merle intones. "They're one
and the same, you know. Both a damn conspiracy to keep
us pacified and in ignorance" (p.133). When she later
meets Saul after returning from communion and he lightly
asks if she has prayed for him, she says, "If I thought
for a moment prayer did any good I'd have prayed for myself." When he persists in urging her to explain her
reasons for going to church, she says, "I don't know why
I go and sit up every Sunday in the damn drafty place.
It doesn't help. Maybe, although I know better, I somehow believe that if I go there often enough and sit
looking at that rose window and listerning to the mumbo
jumbo, a miracle will happen and I'll suddenly find I'm
able to do the one thing I must do if I ever hope to get
moving again" (p.261). For Merle, as for Grange, church
attendance is form without substance and action without
conviction. She is not irreverent, like Grange, nor
does she refuse to attend church, like Mariah. But she
is still not in the fold.

Merle views the church (perhaps more subconsciously
than consciously) as a continuation of the subjugation
she felt with the Englishwoman who tried to reduce her
from person to animal. The violation of self, especially under the guise of Christianity, is intolerable.
Constantly Merle wears a pair of earrings that were the
woman's gift. They are conspicuous adornments: "pendant
silver earrings carved in the form of those saints to be
found on certain European churches.... their tiny faces
gaunt with piety, their eyes closed in prayer" (p.4).
Merle says her patron "had them copied especially for me
from the saints on the outside of Westminster Abbey when
I told her of our hill of the same name" (p.327). With
its religious theme, the symbol represents her "long
subjugation." She wears the earrings throughout her
eight-year sojourn in Bournehills and removes them only
when she is confident of her self-definition. As she is
preparing to leave Bournehills to visit her husband and

daughter, she takes off Mutt and Jeff (the names Saul
has given the earrings).

If Merle is to reach her humanistic potential by
evolving a code of ethics and ending her stagnation, she
cannot embalm herself with religion. That would be a
denial of the human relationships which have brought her
where she is and the ones she must engage in if she is
to live again. In Bournehills, Merle begins to emerge
and to show the potential that will enhance her resolve
to go to Africa. She begins to show traits (perhaps unconsciously at first) that recall the folk tradition and
Cuffee. Initially, she is independent. She lives in
Bournehills instead of in New Bristol, where most of the
educated Bourne Islanders live, and she teaches Bourne
Island history even when it means she will be fired from
her job. She also feels a sense of community with the
people in Bournehills and fights for the "Little Fella,"
a phrase used to describe her neighbors. By choice she
is committed to the people in Bournehills and responsible for them. When the owners of the sugar factory near
Bournehills close it down before the poor people have
ground their canes, Merle goes to the factory, confronts
the foreman, and curses him out for what he represents.

In the Cane Vale sugar factory incident, Merle's commitment to freedom, happiness, and self-determination
illustrates her growth toward an ethic based on her folk
heritage. She is helpless against the forces that own
and operate Cane Vale, but feels that someone must speak
out. The workers are more vulnerable to punishment than
she; having more to lose, they are more afraid. So
Merle voluntarily accepts a responsibility that must
fall on someone's shoulders. If she can only verbalize
the dissatisfaction and the sense of frustration, she
must do that. Accepting responsibility, even though it
brings on a cataleptic state, shows the potential she
has for accepting her actions in England and working to
do something about them.

Her Bournehills experiences help her to appreciate
life's benefits and the individual's effort to realize
them. With its intermingling of past and present,
Bournehills becomes a natural setting for Merle's most
significant move toward freedom. Saul maintains earlier
that history should be used to advantage: "you have to
try and learn from all that's gone before — and again

from both the good and the bad — especially that! Use
your history as a guide, in other words. Because many
times, what one needs to know for the present — the
action that must be taken if a people are to win their
right to live, the methods to be used: some of them un-
palatable, true, but again, there's usually no other way
— has been spelled out in past events. That it's all
there if only they would look..." (p.315).

Merle's history shows self-definition and self-
determination, and she will be free when Bournehills
history merges with hers. She discovers what Saul means
to her personal history when Harriet, Saul's wife, discovers Merle's affair with him. She confronts Merle
with an offer of money to go away. Harriet parallels
the Englishwoman in believing that affection can be
bought and that Merle's affair is reducible to finances.
Given the opportunity to reenact her earlier experiences, to confront her history and learn from it, Merle
vehemently rejects what both Harriet and the Englishwoman represent. By confronting again the force that
would impose a meaning on her life and a definition on
herself, Merle exorcises completely the stagnation that
has resulted from her past experience. The London upheaval in her personal history is as significant as
Cuffee Ned's was to his fellow slaves. Finally, Merle
resists dehumanization. Refusing to be a slave again,
she completes her bid for freedom. She ritualistically
takes off the dangling earrings, symbols of externally
imposed values and definitions for over a decade.

With this act Merle takes on humanism as a guide for
existence. Her effort to define herself, her commitment, and her refusal to be dehumanized place her in the
Cuffee tradition. Human desire and the response to it
bind the two figures, not by any dogmatic or patterned
code. Rather than being imposed upon her, her kinship
to Cuffee has evolved through her actions. She, like
Cuffee, frees herself. As she prepares to leave Bournehills to visit her husband and child, Merle is finally
able to articulate what her newfound freedom means.
Freedom is simply a choice of responsibility and commitment. Merle must go to Africa to try to understand what
motherhood means: "I'll never get around to doing anything with what's left of my life until I go and look
for my child" (p.463). She must acknowledge her role

in her London downfall and deal with the consequences of
that acknowledgment. She can't, she says, go on sitting
around doing nothing and "blaming everyone and everything" for the "botch" she has made of things. Ultimately freedom means a conscious recommitment: "I'll be
coming back to Bournehills. This is home. Whatever
little I can do that will matter for something must be
done here. A person can run for years but sooner or
later he has to take a stand in the place which, for
better or worse, he calls home, do what he can to change
things there" (pp.464,468).

Merle and Bournehills have indeed shared similar experiences. Both experienced upheavals (the London fias-
co for Merle and Cuffee Ned for Bournehills) which left
a similar or seemingly similar stagnation. Her London
adventures stymied Merle, but she has the potential to
grow into her human worth. To the outsider, Bournehills
is a sleepy and backwards district, unprogressive and
stagnant; but underneath are the sure identity and pride
that materialistic outsiders cannot comprehend. There
is room for improvement in Bournehills, but these people
adhere to values interpretable only in terms of their
culture and on their land. Togetherness, mutual responsibility, common goals — these commitments define
Bournehills, and they eventually inspire Merle to shape
her own ethics.

Mariah Upshur and Grange Copeland join Merle Kinbona
in becoming literary models for humanistic living. They
illustrate the process by which one obtains a humanistic
approach to life. Their authors extend that process
from the novels, their self-contained worlds, to that
historical and human world beyond. They use their heritages in folk tradition and their foundations in Black
life to create novels that suggest humanistic processes.
To be humanized by the study of the good arts, Ronald
Crane maintains in *The Idea of the Humanities,* is to be
"endowed with the virtues and knowledge that separate
men most sharply from the lower animals."[7]

An important step in the lives of the characters in
Wright, Walker, and Marshall is that of separating themselves from forces that would dehumanize them. Their
actions are taken by choice. Their love goes beyond bi-
ological factors of kinship; their obligations go beyond

church and state. They recognize no coercions, no re-
quirements except those they assign to themselves. Mariah, Grange, and Merle do not choose simple solutions
to their problems. Their choices show the complexity
and range of human experience, within which they live
as fully as they can. They seek after truth, even when
truth is uncomfortable. The struggles undergone ennoble
them.

With the concentration on Black characters, Wright,
Walker, and Marshall have used a particular instance of
human experience to reflect the peculiarities in man's
nature which race affects rather than limits. With oppression and dehumanization, slavery and its succeeding
oppression provide both synchrony and diachrony. If
the suffering of Blacks does not surpass that of other
races, it was and is more obvious. Taking this obvious
suffering — its historical and social consequences, its
implications — these three writers transcend deterministic-
tic and nihilistic philosophies. The transcendence is
not for the sake of moral lesson, although certainly
lessons might be inferred. But by their independence,
individuality, complexity, and exacting idealisms, the
characters demand more than didactic or cursory considerations. They have a dignity of purpose and ideals
which ultimately demand broad rather than constrictive
evaluation. And the broader evaluation leans toward
a general humanity which goes from brutality to self-
realization.

In a 1973 interview Alice Walker discussed some ob-
jectives that inform her creation of *The Third Life of
Grange Copeland*. Echoing a line from her protagonist,
she says: "I am preoccupied with the spiritual survival,
the survival *whole* of my people."[8]   That wholeness cannot be the psychological stasis of either hating Whites
or setting them up as gods. As Walker explains, religious doctrine cannot sustain human fulfillment.

> I seem to have spent all of my life rebelling against
> the church or other people's interpretations of what
> religion is — the truth is probably that I don't be-
> lieve there is a God, although I would like to be-
> lieve it. Certainly I don't believe there is a God
> beyond nature. The world is God. Man is God. So
> is a leaf or a snake.... So, when Grange Copeland re-
> fuses to pray at the end of the book, he is refusing

to be a hypocrite. All his life he has hated the
Church and taken every opportunity to ridicule it.
He has taught his granddaughter, Ruth, this same humorous contempt. He does, however, appreciate the
humanity of man-womankind as a God worth embracing.
To him, the greatest value a person can attain is
full humanity, which is a state of oneness with all
things, and a willingness to die (or to live) so that
the best that has been produced can continue to live
in someone else. He "rocked himself in his own arms
to a final sleep" because he understood that man is
alone — in his life as in his death — without any God
but himself (and the world).[9]

Paule Marshall joins Walker in this concern. We have
a particular will to survive, Marshall maintains, "And
not only to survive, but to remain responsive, creative
beings whose ability to transform our suffering into art
...attests to the fact that we have kept our humanity
intact.... We are forever transcending our condition.
It is this I want to celebrate."[10]

Yet these writers do not create a race of super
Blacks. They create characters who go on living despite
the degradations faced. These characters show the authors' awareness of complex human situations and the
added complexity coming from oppression. They are good
and bad, victimized and victimizing, enslaved and en-
slaving. Despite their suffering and the suffering they
cause, they hold an inviolable place within themselves
where oppression and the ability to oppress are impo-
tent. They triumph because they define their own reality and their own morality. They live by their choices;
they obligate themselves by standards internally binding. As models of humanistic philosophy, they offer the
serious student of literature a means for gaining knowledge about human kind.

---

[1]Ralph Ellison, *Shadow and Act* (New York: Signet, 1966),
p. 172.
[2]Ibid., p. 173.
[3]Peter Faulkner, *Humanism in the English Novel* (New York:
Harper and Row, 1976), p. 1.

[4]Sarah E. Wright, *This Child's Gonna Live* (New York: Dell/ Delta, 1969).

[5]Alice Walker, *The Third Life of Grange Copeland* (New York: Avon, 1971).

[6]Paule Marshall, *The Chosen Place, The Timeless People* (New York: Harcourt, 1969).

[7]Ronald Crane, *The Idea of the Humanities* (Chicago: Univ. of Chicago Press, 1967), 1: 7.

[8]Alice Walker in *Interviews with Black Writers*, ed. John O'Brien (New York: Liveright, 1973), p. 192.

[9]Ibid., p. 205.

[10]Paule Marshall, "Shaping the World of My Art," *New Letters* 40 (Autumn 1973): 106.

GEORGE E. KENT

Aesthetic Values in the Poetry
of Gwendolyn Brooks

The aesthetic values in Gwendolyn Brooks's poetry emerge
from a close and highly disciplined imitation of the
properties of the objects and situations her art confronts. By imitation I mean here the creative and imaginative engagement of values either actual or possible
in the range of circumstances stirring the mind of the
artist to action. If we are not overtaken by excessive
rigor, we may usefully see the objects and situations
under the following broad headings: existential tensions
confronting any people facing human limitations and possibility; existential tensions given particularism by
styles of engagement, failure, and celebration, created
within Black communities; and the exile rhythms of a
Black people still seeking to establish at-homeness in
America.

Before investigating the listed categories, I must
make some guiding observations. The categories are not
self-isolating compartments, but conveniences for our
discussion; they often fuse with each other. This fusion results from Brooks's determination to present her
people not as curios or exotics but as human beings.
Thus the exile tensions of the famous poem "Negro Hero"[1]
fuse with the existential; on one level the hero is simply adventurous young man, thrilled by his own physical,
mental, and spiritual resources; on another level, he is
the exile possessing an unillusioned hope that his heroic risking of his life in battle will be a step toward
transforming America and ending the exile status. Further, we may occasionally feel impelled to associate

exile tensions with a poem which seems purely involved
with the limitations or triumphs generally afforded in
the human struggle.

The next observation involves the complexity of the
issue of aesthetic values. It cuts across the outlined
categories and affects the total body of the poetry.
Brooks, in her early comments, tended to speak of beauty
and truth as her aims in the creation of poetry. Her
poetry reveals that such qualities are not necessarily
qualities of the aesthetic object or situation, but
qualities of the aesthetic experience afforded by the
form when it is closely engaged. That is, the fusion
of the reader with the work of art in an act of total
perception is the ultimate source of the beauty and the
truth. Thus the primary aesthetic value of a given poem
is in this act of *seeing,* as I have broadly defined it.
Prior to the late 1960s, the outcome of this act of seeing was, primarily, the reader's possession of a revelation admitting him to a deeper human communion. The
poet's turning to a more radical stance during the 1960s
added a more concrete experience of *liberation* to that
of *revelation.* Which is to say that her poetry became
far more attentive to Blacks as an audience than it had
previously. And thus exile and quest for at-homeness
in the universe move to occupy the center of the stage.
But in all the works the reader must expect and engage
an art which sees people as experiencing all the emotions available under the limitations of the human condition, though often without the gilded stage conven-
tionally included to secure us in the illusion of the
automatic omnipresence of human dignity. Whatever dignity and beauty arise from her people must, instead, be
seized from the quality of their struggles and in their
assertion of options despite imposing oppositions.

Such matters may now be more concretely illustrated
and developed by our engagement of specific works of
art. I have chosen these works not to rank the best
poems but to make use of those which, for various reasons, seem most convenient for illustration.

Let's begin, for the existential category, with "the
old-marrieds,"[2] the opening poem of *A Street in Bronzeville* (1945).

> But in the crowding darkness not a word did
>   they say.

> Though the pretty-coated birds had piped so
>   lightly all the day.
> And he had seen the lovers in the little side-
>   streets.
> And she had heard the morning stories clogged
>   with sweets.
> It was quite a time for loving. It was mid-
>   night. It was May.
> But in the crowding darkness not a word did
>   they say.

The form of the poem operates upon our aesthetic perceptions through oppositions which are both stated and
implied. Ostensibly, the oppositions are the behavior
of the couple in the face of conventional symbols of the
time for loving. But perhaps the opposition is also in
our minds, if our response is that this old couple have
simply had it and are exhausted. First, the title suggests a class of people, rather than simply the sad
fate of a particular couple. The images and the phrase
"quite a time for loving" represent rather limited ways
of conceiving loving. Therefore, the poem pushes us into other creations and comparisons — possibly into the
appreciation of the rhythms of human lives which have
achieved a condition wherein there is neither a special
time for loving nor a need for words, and the time for
loving is lifelong. The low-key presentation and the
arrangement of the syntax to give apparent emphasis to
the "proper" time for loving are themselves an incite-
ment to our creative imagination.

Brooks was aware of the artistry and energetic
struggle which go into the so-called ordinary lives of
individuals attempting to ward off chaos and to order
existence. The aesthetic registration of their achieved
possibilities can be laid before us quietly but stroked
permanently into the mind by various poetic devices.
"Southeast corner"[3] achieves its final lift into the
mind and the feelings by a climactic sensuous image:

> The School of Beauty's a tavern now.
> The Madam is underground.
> Out at Lincoln, among the graves
> Her own is early found.
> Where the thickest, tallest monument
> Cuts grandly into the air

The Madam lies, contentedly.
Her fortune, too, lies there,
Converted into cool hard steel
And bright red velvet lining;
While over her tan impassivity
Shot silk is shining.

At one level the poem would seem to fall conclusively
into the category of those impressing us with the vanity
of human gesture and ambition. But the images suggest
powerfully that whatever worms may eventually do, Madam
has had her triumph as artist. With the "tallest monu-
ment" cutting "grandly into the air," the "cool hard
steel" of the casket and its "bright red velvet lining," Madam reaches the climax of her artistic ordering
through the vivid touch of the last line. The image of
shot silk makes a very strong impact through the poet's
use of alliteration and sudden brevity of statement. If
the art Madam has achieved is temporary, it is no more
so than most art.

Brooks recognizes this artistry even when it is cost-
ly to higher levels of the human spirit. "The parents:
people like our marriage, Maxie and Andrew"[4] (*Annie Allen,* 1949) also demands attention to the final climactic
image. In addition there is the contrast between the
image of the people and that of their achievement.

Clogged and soft and sloppy eyes
Have lost the light that bites and terrifies.

There are no swans and swallows any more.
The people settled for chicken and shut the door.

But one by one
They got things done:
Watch for porches as you pass
And prim low fencing pinching in the grass.

Pleasant custards sit behind
The white Venetian blind.

Aesthetically, the poem places upon the reader a creative demand, and one could go on for a few pages describing the synchronized operation of the devices which
deliver its organized energies. But I shall focus upon
merely a few. Perhaps the hardest workers are the
images, and one can feel their impact severally and

contrastingly. "Clogged," "soft," "sloppy eyes" are
notable for their vividness and unlovely suggestion of
decay. The succeeding line announces the focus upon the
loss of spiritual power, with the reader supplying various meanings for "bites and terrifies." Our associations with "swans" and "swallows," in the next couplet,
contrast with those we have for "chicken," usually nothing more than those suggesting good eating. We are
moved from the symbol of the whole, "sloppy eyes," to
the whole which it represents, "the people," that is,
this married couple. And the poet forces us as readers
to answer the question: "shut the door" on what? Once
we have answered it, the next four lines offer dramatic
contrast between loss and achievement by simply describing the couple's achievement ironically in the language
with which we and the neighbors would ordinarily praise
them. The fourth line of this group is notable for
additional registration of the general theme: reduction
of vitality. The last two lines contain the images of
blandness in a triumphantly rising tone, and force a
contrast between this blandness and the surging but lost
human spirit represented by the "light that bites or
terrifies" and by the grace, beauty, and other qualities
associated with swans and swallows.

Thus the poem, in a very brief compass, involves itself in large issues regarding the human condition and
the pathos of human choices. Still, there is a respect
for the couple as artists. That is, they create a form
which brings order and value, however pedestrian, to existence. If the reader has fused with the art construct, he or she should feel a beauty emerging from the
precision of the form in producing the shock of recognition. Intelligence, feelings, psychic responses, and
emotions are aroused through the encounter with a variety of devices. Special note should be taken of the
following: simple but mind-bending imagery, formal
eloquence of language contrasting with the colloquial;
sharp and functional packaging and delivery of thought
and feeling through rhymed couplets; alteration of pace
in various lines to produce appropriate tones.

I have mentioned poems which obviously afford an element of beauty in the act of perception. "The murder"[5]
(*A Street in Bronzeville*), however, offers a different
challenge. The first verse is suggestive.

> This is where poor Percy died,
> Short of the age of one.
> His brother Brucie, with a grin,
> Burned him up for fun.

Three stanzas render Percy's probable responses as he dies, and the final one returns the murderer Brucie to the cocoon of childhood innocence. The aesthetic effects are horror, wonder, and awe, as the artistic construct registers the feeling of the shortness of the distance between childhood innocence and monstrosity. The poem's beginning notes the innocent delight of both boys in the fire, but near the end identifies the monstrosity sometimes lurking behind innocence.

> No doubt, poor shrieking Percy died
> Loving Brucie still,
> Who could, with clean and open eye,
> Thoughtfully kill.

Note the juxtapositions of words embodying both innocence and temporary entrance into monstrosity.

The foregoing may suggest the aesthetic field of the poems in the existential category, but it can hardly indicate the range and the rather large number of Brooks's poems which fall into this classification. It should include such splendid works as the following: several war sonnets registering the struggle of the human spirit against the destructiveness of war (*A Street in Bronzeville*); "the birth in a narrow room," "do not be afraid of no," "Life for my child is simple, and is good," "the children of the poor" (*Annie Allen*); "Strong Men, Riding Horses" and "A Lovely Love" (*The Bean Eaters*); various children's poems;[6] several pieces in the New Poems section of *Selected Poems;*[7] and several poems in such later works as *Riot* and *Beckonings.*[8] These poems reveal the continuity of the poet's art with the rest of existence, and, in their aesthetic values, represent a considerable articulation of varied postures involved in the human experience: the awe-inspiring entrance of the human being into potentially complex existence ("the birth in a narrow room"); the uneasy struggle to retain beauty in the face of war (the war sonnets of "Gay Chaps at the Bar"); the self-validating quality of love without conventional stagings ("A Lovely Love"); various aspects of

love in sundry poems; the complex emotions involved in
motherhood ("the children of the poor" and other poems);
the organization of one's being in the face of life's
enticements to self-betrayal ("do not be afraid of no");
and so on. That the foregoing poems in what I have
called the simply existential category are inspired by
Brooks's intense confrontation with Black life is, for
the pre-1960s era, both an aesthetic and a political
gesture. That is, they achieve her determination to reveal Blacks' participation in the varied complexities of
existence, not as curios but simply as people struggling
to bear their weight in the universe.

The next category of poems is that of those primarily
concerned with the daily round of existence in ordinary
lives but marked by their representation of distinctive
Black styles. Actually, the poet is strongest in ef-
fecting aesthetic values, not in joining the styles to
the existential, but to exile rhythms, as will be seen
later. The foregoing principle tends to apply also to
Black writers in general, the most important exceptions
being numerous poems of Langston Hughes and Sterling A.
Brown. Margaret Walker might be included, with special
reference to her poem "Lineage," in which the rendering
of the strength and life-drive of ancestors evokes a
sense of deep historical rhythms. Such poems seem to
require, if they are not to be superficial or stereo-
typical, transference of value from specific Black folk
forms (spirituals, blues, ballads, for example), or from
images and symbols which continually vibrate with suggestions of historical strivings, or from a few evocative devices which a poet may hit upon.

Brooks's most outstanding attempts in relation to
folk forms, I think, are the popular "of De Witt Williams on his way to Lincoln Cemetery" and "Queen of the
Blues," both included in _A Street in Bronzeville_. The
aesthetic value of "of De Witt Williams..." resides in
the bold celebration of the ordinary life as represented
by a boy who did nothing more than migrate to the North,
gain his measure of enjoyment of the fruits of existence, and pass on to the great beyond. The symbols to
which the reader responds are those representing hang-
out places and typical resources for joy. But ultimate
celebration is suggested by a refrain which implies that
this "ordinary" existence is also graced by the grand

exit described in the spiritual: "Swing low swing low
sweet sweet chariot. / Nothing but a plain black boy."
   "Queen of the Blues" has delightful images and ex-
pressions from the blues singer's tough life in the
urban night, but it seems to me less successful aesthetically. The speaker emphasizes the emotions of compassion and pathos, and regards Mame, the queen of the
blues, as embracing a life of shame opened to her by the
lack of conventional restraints. The queen's story is
the conventional one, without devices for a fresh face-
lifting of the artistic construct. The ultimate problem
is that the poem lacks aesthetic distance from the values of the speaker-poet. "Steam Song"[9] is a more recent
poem which seems to stand sturdily in its own space.

> That Song it sing the sweetness
> like a good Song can
> and make a woman want to
> run out and find her man.
>
> Ain got no pretty mansion.
> Ain got no ruby ring.
> My man is my only
> necessary thing.
>
> That Song boil up my blood
> like a good Song can
> It make this woman want to
> run out and find her man.

   In a number of poems, the poet satirizes the presentations of the hip-style, but the strongest treatment
of the style appears in critical conjunction with exile
rhythms in "The Sundays of Satin Legs Smith" (*A Street
in Bronzeville*). Besides the foregoing types of poems,
Brooks has others which evoke identification of poetic
style with Blackness, often by a single word or phrase
or through voice tones and familiar images which would
be seen as involving Blacks.
   "A song in the front yard" clearly concerns the tensions between the style of Black respectability and the
more spontaneous life of the less respectable. The name
Johnnie Mae would suggest to the Black reader the racial
identity of the subjects. Names and the label "thin
brown mouse" for the colleged Maud in "Sadie and Maud"
make the identification of the respectable and wilder

styles racially clear, but the zing of style is suggested by such an expression as "Sadie was one of the
livingest chits / In all the land." Aesthetically, in
these lighthearted poems from *A Street in Bronzeville,*
the poet poses in tension the values of the ordered existence and those of the less restrained.

Another aspect of Black style is represented by the
Hattie Scott poems[10] (*A Street in Bronzeville*), portraits of the coping spirit of an ordinary domestic
worker. They present incisive portrayals of her responses to existence in relationship to work, love,
beauty, and man-woman associations. Their aesthetic
value resides in artistic constructs which register a
day-to-day heroism. In the first of this series, "the
end of the day," Hattie identifies herself with the sun:
"But the sun and me's the same, could be: / Cap the job,
then to hell with it." In the second, "the date," she
is grumblingly ready to transcend the oppressive gestures of her domestic employer by boldly departing for
her evening on the town with her date: "I'm leavin'.
Got somethin' interestin' on my mind. / Don't mean night
school." In the third (at the hairdresser's"), she
triumphs over her difficulties with the competing girls
of long and wind-blown hair. The last two verses illustrate the poet's mastery of her character's voice tones.

> Got Madam C. J. Walker's first.
> Got Poro Grower next.
> Ain't none of 'em worked with me, Min.
> But I ain't vexed.
>
> Long hair's out of style anyhow, ain't it?
> Now it's tie it up high with curls.
> Gimme an upsweep, Minnie.
> I'll show them girls.

The fourth and fifth poems strike the hard, folk,
cynical note, with Hattie picturing the brevity with
which her lover will mourn her passing and the violence
with which she would have repelled the whipping her
friend Moe Belle Jackson so humbly accepted from her
husband. In such later volumes as *Annie Allen* (1949)
and *The Bean Eaters* (1960), Brooks continued such ex-
plorations but tended to edge them with satire or humor.
Style portraits appear, too, in *In the Mecca,*[11] but they

derive some of their impact from being in a setting
created by exile rhythms. Although the exile rhythms
are not always directly presented in other later works
dealing with individual Black styles and incorporation
of African ones (*Family Pictures,* 1970; *Beckonings,*
1975), they are sufficiently registered by other poems
within the book to provide a carry-over impact.

In approaching the final category of the poems,
those dealing with exile rhythms, I wish to repeat that
the word exile means here a people experiencing resistance to their desire for at-homeness in the universe
of their native land, and seeking firm establishment
of it. Brooks's mode for communicating these exile
tensions in the pre-1960s differs from that of the late
1960s through the 1970s. Rightly this difference in
modes raises the question of audience, since audience
is a central shaping factor in the selection and registration of aesthetic values.

To avoid the superficial commentary by which one
usually explores the question of audience and to be
brief simultaneously, I must express the situation prag-
matically. As sometimes theorized, the artist, moved by
something called "the human condition," pauses in his or
her arrangements of rhythms to inquire, "Who's out there
listening?" Prior to the 1960s those declaring their
attention to Brooks would be a large number of Whites
and a small number of Blacks. The Whites' answer would
express interest in the universal and a disinclination
to read about problems. There would also be, from many,
unstated premises or doubts regarding the Blacks' humanity outside special exotic categories. Thus the
question, "Is your work about Negroness or about the
human condition?" would suggest unstated premises. By
the time of World War II, within the answer of the small
number of Blacks reading Black poetry or any poetry,
would also be the expression of interest in the universal, but without the qualifications or unstated premises or doubts regarding Blacks' humanity. Perhaps the
titles of articles appearing in an issue of the magazine
Phylon during 1950, which was devoted to the theme "The
Negro in Literature: The Current Scene," sufficiently
suggest the thrusts of Blacks' interest: Gwendolyn
Brooks, "Poets Who Are Negro"; Lewis G. Chandler, "A
Major Problem of Negro Authors in Their March Toward

Belle Lettres"; Thomas Jarrett, "Toward Unfettered Creativity"; and others. White critical articles or reviews
reflected happiness when they could assure the reading
public that the artistic construct transcended racial
categories and racial protest. But, somewhat paradoxically, they also insisted upon the art construct's in-
formative role, by asserting that the Black artist was
telling us what it meant to be a Negro.

Gwendolyn Brooks and writers from Gustavus Vassa
to the present, however, were not simply molded by the
foregoing expectations. The fact that when we do read
earlier Black works we emerge with a strong sense of
profit shows that most serious artists forcefully made
their own integrity an important element of their works.
Richard Wright's letter to his editor Edward C. Aswell
urging publication of Brooks's first book, *A Street in
Bronzeville,* illustrates the point. Says Wright regarding the poems:

> They are hard and real, right out of the central core
> of Black Belt Negro life in urban areas.... There is
> no self-pity here, nor a striving for effects. She
> takes hold of reality as it is and renders it faith-
> fully. [The next sentence is bracketed, evidently by
> Wright's editor, or another Harpers editor.] There
> is not so much an exhibiting of Negro life to whites
> in these poems as there is an honest human reaction
> to the pain that lurks so colorfully in the Black
> Belt. A quiet but hidden malice runs through most
> of them.[12]

Much of the remainder of the letter stresses the poems'
integrity and the artist's, as well as a plea that she
be helped at all costs.

Perhaps I can suggest the complexity of audience and
its impact upon the rendering of aesthetic values by
pointing out the following. The response of the artist
to the pre-1960s audience and her own convictions produced signals and rhythms representing an intricate and
complex imaging and revelation of Black experience. The
response of the larger Black audience after the mid-
1960s to the question of who's listening out there was
loudly, "We are, and we want everything which will move
our condition." Responding from the heart, the poet in-
fused images and symbols into the art construct which

emphasized liberation rather than representation and
revelation only. The trademark of all her poetry, however, is a firm registration of existential rhythms
operating in tension with all other emphases. I now
turn to samples representing exile rhythms in works from
both before and after the mid-1960s.

In order to deal with so important and extensive a
body of poetry, I shall have to add some shorthand techniques to my method. First, the exile rhythms may arise
from either interracial or intraracial prejudice. Second, qualities of the objects of art (the Blacks and ac-
companying situations) may be broadly characterized as
follows: the spirit downed or reduced but not defeated
("kitchenette building" and others in *A Street in
Bronzeville*); the spirit corrupted ("Jessie Mitchell's
Mother" in *The Bean Eaters*); the spirit's movement into
isolation after assertion of human value ("the ballad of
chocolate Mabbie," "Ballad of Pearl May Lee," "The Sundays of Satin-Legs Smith" in *A Street in Bronzeville*);
the spirit stoically holding on despite assault ("The
Last Quatrain of the Ballad of Emmett Till" in *The Bean
Eaters;* "To a Winter Squirrel" in *In the Mecca*); and the
largely individual or special group spirit in the act
of heroic assertion ("Negro Hero" and "the white troops
had their orders but the Negroes looked like men" in *A
Street in Bronzeville;* "The Ballad of Rudolph Reed" in
The Bean Eaters; various personalities in "In the Mecca"
in the book of the same title). *In the Mecca* (1968) is
transitional. The long poem "In the Mecca" represents
a transition to the focus upon liberation. Since the
poems in the section "After Mecca" are a movement toward
liberation values, I leave them for the second part of
this discussion.

Still another group of poems represents Blacks in the
act of perception of Whites, in which Whites or their
patterns of behavior also become art objects. Those
representing Blacks and the poet as self-contained and
cultivated observers are such poems as "Beverly Hills,
Chicago," "I love those little booths at Benvenuti's,"
"downtown vaudeville," "Men of careful turns, haters of
forks in the road," all in *Annie Allen;* "A Bronzeville
Mother Loiters in Mississippi. Meanwhile, a Mississippi
Mother Burns Bacon" and "The Chicago *Defender* Sends a
Man to Little Rock" in *The Bean Eaters*. Perhaps "The

Sundays of Satin-Legs Smith" should also be mentioned
among the foregoing group; although the portrait of the
Black character dominates that poem, the real cool Black
observer makes her first appearance in it. To many of
today's readers the foregoing poems are likely to be
seen as containers of polite protest. But Whites experienced from most of them considerable bite; the poet
was queried as to why she was bitter and why she was
"forsaking lyricism for polemics." The reason for their
impact is not hard to discover. The narrator speaks
not as one whose wounds and howls can be addressed by
a single moment of pity, but as one for the most part
containing his or her pain and speaking as the equal
capable of staring eye for eye and delivering rapier
thrusts.

The more bitter and more dramatically slashing poems
of this group are "Negro Hero" (*A Street in Bronzeville*), and "Bronzeville Woman in a Red Hat" and "The
Lovers of the Poor" (*The Bean Eaters*). (It should be
said that other categories, such as that of heroic assertion, also contain bitterly slashing poems.) These
poems address issues of dignity and brotherhood. In the
short epic "In the Mecca," as distinguished from the
book which contains it, the appearance of personalities
bent upon revolutionary change signals the approaching
end to the formerly implied hope for change through in-
tergroup cooperation.

"Kitchenette building" renders its sense of the
reduction of the spirit of a people, crowded and impov-
erished in urban housing, mainly by the impact of contrasting images of concrete struggle for existence with
those representing aspirations and dreams. Most obvious
are the overripe odors of the struggle to maintain mini-
mal dignity for body and spirit as contrasted with the
level of life suggested by the music of an aria. But
in addition there is the contrast between colors: the
grayed life of the people versus the "white and violet"
of aspiration and dream. The poem, however, should be
compared with "when you have forgotten Sunday: the love
story" in which the married couple creatively manage a
triumph of the human spirit over circumstances.

As noted earlier, "The Sundays of Satin-Legs Smith"
joins the exile rhythms with an enactment and a criticism of hip Black style. The tendency of some readers

is to ignore the criticism and merely to enjoy the
nostalgic recollection of Smith's representation of a
colorful period. The poem celebrates his powerful assertion of a sense of the beautiful through clothes, a
highly styled behavior which permits withdrawal to self-
gratifying indulgences, including the absolute value he
places upon sex. But it comes down hard on the short-
comings of Smith and the addressed White observer whose
oppression has reduced the reach for beauty and evoked
a response of grotesqueness. The public voice makes the
situation clear, and the poet's private voice, with compassion, underlines the criticism of Smith.

> People are so in need, in need of help.
> People want so much that they do not know.
>
> Below the tinkling trade of little coins
> The gold impulse not possible to show
> Or spend. Promise piled over and betrayed.

Full rendering of Smith's artistry is accompanied by
some of the complex irony with which the poem abounds.
In the following passage, the extraordinary management
of tone renders both the rhythms of Smith's triumphant
gestures and a suggestion of his limitations.

> These kneaded limbs receive the kiss of silk.
> Then they receive the brave and beautiful
> Embrace of some of that equivocal wool.
> He looks into his mirror, loves himself —
> The neat curve here; the angularity
> That is appropriate at just its place;
> The technique of a variegated grace.

Later, the poet's tone is direct in characterizing
Smith's limitations: "The pasts of his ancestors lean
against / Him. Crowd him. Fog out his identity."
And finally, the lyric ending of the poem ironically
enforces the reader's realization of Smith's failure
as artist of his existence. The reach for the absolute
is usually thought of as a reach for the supreme spirit
of the universe: Smith's is for the most physical sen-
sations of sex only:

> *Her body is like new brown bread*
> *Under the Woolworth mignonette.*

> *Her body is a honey bowl*
> *Whose waiting honey is deep and hot.*
> *Her body is like summer earth,*
> *Receptive, soft, and absolute...*

Note the effect of the mixture of images and the repetition of "her body." Still Smith, in his rituals of
expression, which are really rituals of isolation from
the richer elements of existence, "Judges he walks most
powerfully alone, / That everything is — simply what it
is."

"Satin-Legs" is an excellent example of a poem in
which the poet seems to work fully all the rhythms and
significance applicable to the human space occupied
by her subject. Although technically the poem runs a
contrast between White expectations and Black reality,
the reader's realization that all images of highest
aspiration are in White terms is unsettling: Grieg,
Tschaikovsky, "the shapely tender drift of Brahms."

No such issue arises with respect to other categories
or in other poems with the same theme of the character's
movement into isolation. "The ballad of chocolate Mabbie," a poem in which the heroine is pushed into spiritual isolation by intraracial prejudice against dark
skin, drives home its pathos by the simple lines "Mabbie
on Mabbie with hush in the heart. / Mabbie on Mabbie to
be." Among the heroic poems, the poise of the Black
soldiers in "the white troops had their orders" remains
as an undisturbed image. Long after one has experienced
the poem, the "Negro hero" of the piece by that title
remains memorable for several reasons: the sophisticated
use of sound values, the achievement of various speech
tones by the speaker, rich imagery which serves ironic
purposes, wit, and the tension between the existential
self of the hero and his role as soldier. The title
character of "The Ballad of Rudolph Reed" is made memorable by the metaphor of "oakening" as he lays down
his life in defiance of the Whites who would destroy
his family and home. His wife also stands out coura-
geously in the final lines:

> Small Mabel whimpered all night long,
> For calling herself the cause.
> Her oak-eyed mother did no thing
> But change the bloody gauze.

In "To a Winter Squirrel," a poem in which a victimized
young woman admires the resources of the squirrel and
considers her own limitations, the image of the woman's
spirit is driven home in the second verse: "...Merdice /
of murdered heart and docked sarcastic soul, / Merdice
/ the bolted nomad, on a winter noon / cooks guts; and
sits in gas...." The squirrel lives in its meaning for
Merdice: "She thinks you are a mountain and a star, un-
baffleable; / with sentient twitch and scurry."

The poems in which the emphasis is upon Blacks perceiving Whites, from the point of view of the artist's
intentions, offer no serious problems in the expression
of bitter criticism. Such poems are intentionally a
bitter satire upon White pretensions. Problems occur
in the more restrained poems when the Black observer
becomes too cool, too detached, too oblivious of the
immediately historical pressures in a jet-speed trip to
the universal, or too pleading. Those fully achieved
aesthetically, I would suggest, are three poems from
Annie Allen: "Beverly Hills, Chicago," in its portrait
of Blacks abashed by the contrast between their poverty
and the material comfort and grace of White styles of
living; "I love those little booths," describing Whites
disappointed in their expectations of the exotic behavior of Blacks; and "downtown vaudeville," presenting
the superciliousness of Whites confronting the art of
a Black performer.

On the other hand, "Men of Careful Turns" (*Annie Allen*), a poem attacking the idea of gradualism in race
relations, loses dignity as the observer-narrator pleads
to be included in the regular round of human communion.
"A Bronzeville Mother" (*The Bean Eaters*) has pleased
many because of the poet's stance of considering a White
woman, who was the source of the lynching of an early
adolescent Black boy, simply as mother. In doing so,
the poet ignores the grotesque historical conditions
which the heroine would have to work through before ex-
emplifying the humanity with which she is endowed. "The
Chicago *Defender*" (*The Bean Eaters*) also leaps over historical rhythms in order to get as quickly as possible
to the universal — and thus sidesteps the nasty rhythms
in the experience of attempting to integrate the schools
in Little Rock, Arkansas.

The long poem "In the Mecca" gathers up the evidence

of the exile status of Blacks in order to balance it
against the older hopes for resolution through simple
human awareness. Hopes cannot rise on the scale provided by the poem. The story creating the framework of
"In the Mecca" is that of Mrs. Sally returning to her
numerous family from galling domestic work to discover
finally her youngest child murdered by a warped man
named Jamaica Eddie. With the other stories and portraits occasioned by the encounters with occupants of
the huge Mecca apartment building, Mrs. Sally enforces
the sense of a lost people in a lost or abandoned universe. Yet in many there are hidden beauty, tragic
rhythms, charm, an awareness of profound human values.
The voices of thwarted or simply hidden or confused
lives are accompanied by those seeking clarity and
others giving images of violent revolution. Usually the
poet's voice is simply for humanness. The images of all
people in this universe are incisive, hard, concrete.
The apartment area and building are themselves concrete and definite in their symbolism. Indeed, so much
power has been generated that a justifiable complaint,
aesthetically speaking, is that it cannot be contained
by the poem's ending: a beautiful dirge for the murdered
Pepita which allows for a termination on the notes of
pathos and compassion. The poet Alfred, one of the
poem's speakers, seems closer to the right ending note:

> something, something in Mecca
> continues to call! Substanceless, yet like
>   mountains,
> like rivers and oceans too; and like trees
> with wind whistling through them. And steadily
> an essential sanity, black and electric,
> builds to a reportage and redemption.
>   A hot estrangement.
>   A material collapse
> that is Construction.

The next poems are involved not with representation
or revelation only, but with the values of liberation.
Leaving to others elaborate political pronouncements,
elaborate get-Whitey strategies, and free-wheeling
suggestions of violence, Brooks seized largely upon
cultivation of group and intragroup self-appreciation,
togetherness, creativity, endurance, wisdom, and faith,

for the liberation values to be pushed. Here her first
examples of strong achievement are those involving the
portrayal of personalities (Merdice of "To a Winter
Squirrel"; the anonymous boy of "Boy Breaking Glass" in
In the Mecca) and such heroes as Medgar Evers and Malcolm X. These poems allowed for the exercise of the
artistic reflexes which Brooks had been cultivating over
the years, the results of which are frequently poems
whose linguistic subtleties would confuse the mass audience of Blacks she found it mandatory to reach. Note
the second verse of "Medgar Evers."

> Old styles, old tempos, all the engagement of
> the day — the sedate, the regulated fray —
> the antique light, the Moral rose, old gusts,
> tight whistlings from the past, the mothballs
> in the Love at last our man foreswore.

Of these lines in "Malcolm X": "a sorcery devout and
vertical / beguiled the world." Here the poems are well
conceived, achieved, and finished, nonetheless. And I'm
not always sure of the judgment we make regarding what
a mass audience can understand — especially a people who
made so much out of complex biblical books. But it is
clear that the path to the people requires watchfulness
regarding self-conscious literary formalisms.

Whereas the foregoing poems are achieved, those about
the street gang and its members sometimes suggest the
need for a longer stage of conceptualization or another
kind of execution. Many hoped that street gangs, with
their presumed ability to see through establishment values, would turn to love and liberation values in behalf
of their communities, but the historical record will
probably show that such turnings, given the nature of
street gangs, are not easily to be anticipated. In
"Gang Girls" (*In the Mecca*), the poet engaged gang realities closely, found the girls to be captive souls whose
sacrifice was great. The poet reveals the situation but
neither indicates responsible parties nor makes a relationship with liberation.

Brooks's next three pamphlet-like books began to be
more suggestive regarding the aesthetics of her newer
approach to audience. The title poem of *Riot* (1969)
suggests a movement toward a more straight-line simplicity, though words continue to work for complex sug-

gestion. The other poems in the volume maintain the
simplicity of the first poem, and one of them, "An Aspect of Love, Alive in the Ice and Fire," has the ma-
jestic finish which one experiences with the earlier
work. *Family Pictures* (1970)[13] and *Beckonings* (1975)
confirm that simplicity, a hardworking but less complex
diction, and further negotiations with folk forms and
their values increasingly form a part of her emerging
system. Besides the difficulty posed by the necessity
to change old artistic habits, the poet faced a rather
fluid political situation and changing responses of
Blacks to it. The titles of the three little books are
significant regarding such changes. *Family Pictures*
suggests at-homeness among friends, but *Beckonings* suggests that the poet must now point to the areas where
values must be developed and maintained. This role is
likely to make the development of the poet's newer
aesthetic an even greater struggle, since it frequently
demands artistic constructs that are admonitory, horta-
tory, and prophetic — roles which threaten to become
enveloped in abstract terms. We have seen, however,
that Brooks's great gift is the concrete. And the poems
of *Beckonings* show that she is aware of such threats and
is preparing to meet them.

On the liberation poems, it is difficult to be more
than tentative. But the will and commitment which created the earlier poems will also probably effect its
triumph in this category. How great a triumph? Only
the future can tell.

---

[1]Gwendolyn Brooks, "Negro Hero," *A Street in Bronzeville* in
The World of Gwendolyn Brooks (New York: Harper and Row, 1971),
pp. 32-34. (This volume reprints *A Street in Bronzeville*
[1945], *Annie Allen* [1949], *Maude Martha* [1953], *The Bean
Eaters* [1960], and *In the Mecca* [1968],) Hereafter cited as
World.

[2]Ibid., p. 3.

[3]Ibid., p. 7.

[4]Ibid., p. 70.

[5]Ibid., p. 22.

[6]*Bronzeville Boys and Girls* (New York: Harper and Row,
1956); *Aloneness* (Detroit: Broadside, 1971); and *The Tiger Who
Wore White Gloves* (Chicago: Third World Press, 1974).

[7]*Selected Poems* (New York: Harper and Row, 1963).

[8]*Riot* (Detroit: Broadside, 1969); *Beckonings* (Detroit: Broadside, 1975).

[9]*Beckonings,* p. 8.

[10]*World,* pp. 35–39.

[11]Ibid., pp. 376–403.

[12]Richard Wright to Edward C. Aswell, September 18, 1944, in Gwendolyn Brooks File, Harper and Row, New York, N.Y.

[13]*Family Pictures* (Detroit: Broadside, 1970).

R. BAXTER MILLER

"Does Man Love Art?":
The Humanistic Aesthetic
of Gwendolyn Brooks

Humanism has long characterized the poetry of Gwendolyn
Brooks. Since *A Street in Bronzeville* (1945) she has
varied the forms of Shakespearean and Petrarchan sonnets; especially since *The Bean Eaters* (1960) she has
experimented with free verse and social theme. For more
than thirty years she has excelled in the skills of alliteration, balance, plosive, and rhetorical question.
Against a background of light and dark, her techniques
reveal a deeply human struggle. Her world evokes death,
history, pain, sickness, identity, and life; her personae seek the grace and vision of personal style. Although her forms vary, her poems generally impose order
upon "the flood of chaos."[1] Are the creations ambivalent? Does form sublimate the personality as well as
reveal it? Did Keats correctly desire "negative capa-
bility" and discern Shakespeare's greatness?

Appreciation of the paradox gives poetry power and
meaning. Humanism is the personally cultural medium
for seeking and defining knowledge, ethical value, and
aesthetics. Through subjectivity the living writer
inspires the inanimate poem. Conversation anthropo-
centrically signifies the speaker. Written language,
rather, implies first an autonomous narrator and second
an historical author. Humanism is the instrument for
creating and interpreting signs. The method opposes
society to self, environment to heredity, death to life,
horizontality to verticality, formalism (science) to

mythmaking, and barbarism to civilization. By humanism, characters experience choice, empathy, love, style, identity, and need. Humanism represents both the relative and the absolute, and Brooks portrays the tension between the two (her whirlwind) where one struggles for stasis within flux.

Her attempts place Western art forms and artists in a Black folk perspective. At different times her speakers refer to baroque and rococo styles in architecture and to traditional musicians — Saint-Saëns, Brahms, Grieg, or Tschaikovsky. Pablo Picasso appears at least once in her poetry. But these images have counterparts. Satin-Legs Smith and a Black youth rioting in the streets are common people. Even Langston Hughes becomes an ironic means for rehumanizing what F. R. Leavis has called the Great Tradition. By demonstrating the inseparability of objective and subjective art, Brooks frees the tradition from itself. Her formal style creates a poetic world in which a folk view contrasts with an elite one, although class differences obscure a common bond. Here one culture's destruction is another culture's creation, so there is a need to redefine culture itself.

Brooks's personae live somewhere between determinism and personal choice. The artist signifies the reader, his human relative; he represents history and collectivity as well as creative process. Using this framework to portray both narrator and artist as hero and heroine, the poet verifies the importance of his or her personal struggle. Here I describe Brooks's humanistic aesthetic. First, she charts its fall from meaning to meaninglessness in early and more stylized poems such as "The Sundays of Satin-Legs Smith" and "still do I keep my look, my identity..." (*A Street in Bronzeville*); second, she develops the aesthetic through a middle stage characterized by distance, alienation, and continued questioning in the second sonnet of *Annie Allen* (1949); third, she forcibly reaffirms the principle in freer forms such as "Langston Hughes" (*Selected Poems*, 1963), or "Boy Breaking Glass" and "The Chicago Picasso" (*In the Mecca* 1968).[2]

"Satin-Legs" posed early the existential question which was to concern Brooks for more than thirty years. As with later poems, such as number XV in *Annie Allen*

and "Second Sermon on the Warpland" in *Mecca*, it sets
style and imagination against a deterministic reality
and asks if they can prevail. In *Annie* the answer is
maybe; in "Second Sermon," a presupposed yes; in "Satin-
Legs," no. "Satin-Legs" can be conveniently divided
into three parts. The first (ll. 1-42) describes a folk
character who rises from bed one morning in Black Chicago and gets dressed. Some sweet scents ironically
suggest his royalty and contrast sharply with his im-
poverished environment. The resulting tensions indirectly show the relative beauty of roses, dandelions,
and garbage. The second part (ll. 43-74) illustrates a
common journey by narrator and reader into Satin-Legs's
closet, a metaphor of man. Here the wide shoulder pad-
ding representing Satin-Legs's sculpture and art contrasts with the baroque and rococo styles, European
forms of the seventeenth and eighteenth centuries. In
the third part (ll. 75-158) ear and eye imagery reveal
Satin-Legs's unawareness of the world about him, as
clothing helps to suggest human deprivation. The narrative movement leads first from the speaker's original
antagonism toward her listener ("you") to a light epic
concerning Satin-Legs's wardrobe. Following the dis-
appearance of "you" from the poem, the narrator finally
views Satin-Legs from a lonely detachment. Ironically
this last section juxtaposes blues with the European
classics of the late nineteenth century and simultaneously shows that cultural values are relative.[3] In a
final irony Satin-Legs ends each Sunday sleeping with
a different prostitute.[4]

The human dimension in the first part, more narrowly
confined, first depends upon animal imagery (Satin-Legs,
the elaborate cat), then upon the metaphor of life's
drama (getting dressed), and last upon the irony characterizing social code ("prim precautions"). An oxymoron
communicates Satin-Legs's confusion ("clear delirium"),
yet the phrase clarifies a double consciousness working
in the poem where the narrator's thinking occasionally
merges with that of Satin-Legs. Whereas his perspective
is generally muddled, hers is usually clear. Applying
some theories of Noam Chomsky, Lévi-Strauss, and Jacques
Derrida stimulates two questions. First, what unifies
Satin-Legs with his narrator? Second, what does the
narrator share with the listener whom George Kent (in

his essay) calls White? Unconsciously Satin-Legs wants
to re-search his limited life and his deferred human potential in order to redefine life's meaning. At first
he temporarily succeeds when the narrator's words reveal
his consciousness: "...life must be aromatic. / There
must be scent, somehow there must be some."[6] His clothing style and cologne merely translate beauty into different kinds of imagery, either visual or olfactory.
Conceptions of art, ideal in nature, are universal; but
their manifestations, their concrete realities, differ.
With a playful tone, the narrator begins her journey
which leads through aloofness and sarcasm to sympathetic
judgment. En route she ironically opposes the cultural
transformations of humanity to humanity itself.

The final two stanzas in the first part firmly establish the opposition. Would the "you," the narrator
questions, "deny" Satin-Legs his scent of lavender and
pine? What substitute would the listener provide? In
a recent article on Brooks's *In the Mecca,* I observe
that Brooks alludes to the Biblical passage in which God
speaks to his afflicted servant Job out of the whirlwind.[7] The observation pertains here because the same
chapter ends with God's inquiring, "Who provideth for
the raven his food?" (Job 38:41). Whereas in "Satin-
Legs" the narrator asks the listener if he can be God,
the speaker in "Second Sermon" secularizes God's command: "Live and go out. / Define and / medicate the
whirlwind." An overall difference separates Satin-Legs,
who needs an external definition for his life, from the
speaker who in "Second Sermon" both demonstrates and demands self-definition.

Coming after 1967, "Second Sermon" characterized a
later period when Brooks's concern for a White audience
lessened and her voice became more definite. "Satin-
Legs," in contrast, shows a more introspective and questioning tone. Should Smith have flowers, the speaker
asks, good geraniums, formal chrysanthemums, magnificent
poinsettias and beautiful roses "in the best / Of taste
and straight tradition"? While bolstering the narrator's sensitivity, the images prepare for the inquiry as
to whether a common humanity can exist: "But you forget,
or did you ever know, / His heritage of cabbage and pig-
tails...." Here the poem implies some questions. Is
oppression both synchronic and diachronic? When does

one's perception shift from momentary to universal time?
How do race and class transform the perception? For the
speaker such unstated queries are secondary because the
listener's desire for knowledge must precede their being
asked. After the narrator describes Smith as being
flowerless, except for a feather in his lapel, she relates dandelions to death. But for whom?

> You [the reader] might as well —
> Unless you care to set the world a-boil
> And do a lot of equalizing things,
> Remove a little ermine, say, from kings,
> Shake hands with paupers and appoint them men,
> For instance — certainly you might as well
> Leave him [Smith] his lotion, lavender and oil.

For Brooks's narrator and the reader, to "shake hands
with paupers and appoint them men" is to perceive that
worth and happiness are human rights, not social priv-
ileges. And the poem's listener must accept the responsibility required by the understanding in order to
participate fully in the aesthetic experience.

The second part of "Satin-Legs" educates the reader
by representing Smith as humanity's icon and its need to
create art. Form, as a motif, unifies Smith's clothes
style as described in the first part with the literary
styles of the sixteenth and seventeenth centuries, as
well as with the architectural styles of the seventeenth
and eighteenth centuries. "Let us" signals the simul-
taneous entry by the narrator and the reader into the
"innards" of Smith's closet, a journey not into his
wardrobe alone but into the human heart. His closet,
a vault, lacks those diamonds, pearls, and silver plate
which characterize the modern upper class. When addressed earlier to a speaker's coy mistress, Andrew
Marvell's lines imply a more genteel tone: "Thy beauty
shall no more be found, / Nor, in thy marble vault,
shall sound / My echoing song...."[8] Brooks subtly par-
odies Anglo-American poetry, for to transpose "vault"
from the pastoral world to the urban one is to retrace
Anglo-American and African literature to their anthro-
pomorphic center. In her only direct intrusion, the
narrator interrupts: "People are so in need, in need of
help. / People want so much that they do not know." By
their directness the lines bridge the aesthetic distance

which separates Satin-Legs from his speaker. Yet the
closure accentuates human time, the rupture between the
flawed medium of language and the mythic ideal which
evokes language. Language can only signify myth, and
the discrepancy between the two represents the difference between the real and the ideal. Paradoxically the
poem becomes a linguistic object which divides Smith
from his narrator; its language separates its reader
from both, even while simultaneously involving the reader. The aesthetic experience becomes grotesque for the
same reason Smith's wardrobe finally does. The weakness
of all art forms and styles lies in their absolute ob-
jectification, for only humanness can invest art with
meaning.

By contrasting Black folk style with traditional
style, the last three stanzas of the second part illustrate the theme. Dressed in silk and wool, Smith looks
self-lovingly into his mirror, "The neat curve here; the
angularity / That is appropriate at just its place; /
The technique of a variegated grace." In expanding the
range of characterization, Brooks re-searches[9] the tradition of Anglo-American poetry and finds an ontological
justification for freeing the tradition from itself.
Her means is still parody, but this time the writer par-
odied is less Marvell than Shakespeare. Written more
than three centuries before, the bard's fifty-fifth sonnet associates a lover's affections with marble and
stone. By intensity, however, love outshines and out-
lasts these substances: "When wasteful war shall statues
overturn, / And broils root out the work of masonry, /
Nor Mars his sword nor war's quick fire shall burn / The
living record of your memory." Brooks, by contrast,
writes about Smith: "Perhaps you would prefer to this a
fine / Value of marble, complicated stone. / Would have
him think with horror of baroque, / Rococo. You forget
and you forget." The Shakespearean type, literary form
here, prepares for Brooks's later description of architectural design. Baroque represents the elaborate and
ornate forms of the seventeenth century while rococo
signifies the curved, fanciful, and spiralled forms of
the eighteenth. Brooks, however, re-places these styles
in the wide pattern of human creativity where Smith
belongs. For twentieth-century America, her narrator
shows, Western humanism's foundation in the Italian and

English Renaissance is paradoxical, for even Shakespeare
spoke about the "living record," a testimony not of empirical history but of personal engagement. Brooks's
Smith is pathetically blameworthy because he has style
without the living memory. But a true imagination must
fuse the aesthetic object with life.

The third part of the poem, the journey into the
world shows that Smith lacks a true imagination. At
Joe's Eats he dines with a different prostitute each
Sunday.[10] He is not, as George Kent observes, the artist of his existence. Obsessed with sex, he has come to
accept the distinction between subjective and objective
reality. Having first admired him, the narrator now
stands more distantly away. Determinism has overcome
the personal flamboyancy which opposed it. Heroic Man,
who organizes by art, has deteriorated into Absurd Man,
who stands apart from it.[11] Smith and the narrator exchange places; her irony and her judgment become more
severe.

The dramatic reversal, as Aristotle calls it, is
slow. When Smith dances down the steps, his movement,
an art form, reminds the reader of Smith's getting
dressed earlier. But basking in sunlight and drinking
coffee at breakfast merely obscure his lost awareness:
"He hears and does not hear / The alarm clock meddling
in somebody's sleep; / ... / An indignant robin's reso-
lute donation.... / He sees and does not see the broken
windows." The robin unhappily sings its song, as Smith
"designed" his "reign" before. Its song symbolically
typifies the human assertion which develops first from
poem XV in *Annie Allen,* next through the short poems
"Langston Hughes" and "Big Bessie throws her son into
the street" in *Selected Poems,* finally in "Second Sermon" in *In the Mecca.* In both of the latter volumes,
Big Bessie appears at the end because she typologically
combines infirmness with endurance.

Smith, however, lacks Big Bessie's complex vision.
Although he is the narrator's means for revealing many
styles, he cannot recognize that his own flair conceals
his sordid environment. He overlooks the wear of a little girl's ribbons and the certain hole that underlies a
little boy's neat patch. Socially blind, he ignores the
women who return from church to their homes on Sunday.
Perceiving them clearly would help him to illuminate his

own identity, since their lives illustrate the inseparability of determinism and personal choice. Their social
conditions have partially governed whether their service
is to God, to those well-off people requiring domestics,
or to men's carnality. Verbal play contributes to an
overall structure in which music now replaces architecture, although both media demonstrate cultural subjectivity. Smith loiters in the street where he hears
"The Lonesome Blues, the Long-lost Blues." In imagining
Saint-Saëns, Grieg, Tschaikovsky, and Brahms, the speaker asks, "could he love them?" The four composers represent France (Western Europe), Norway (Northern Europe), Russia (Eastern Europe), and Germany (Central
Europe). When considered together they form almost a
graphic structure of the continent. All lived in the
nineteenth century, and only Grieg (d. 1907) among the
three lived into the twentieth. Why does the poem show
temporal stasis here when the second part showed a progression from the sixteenth century to the eighteenth?
Trying to resolve his historical identity, for Smith,
compels first an explanation of his cultural self. His
musical aesthetic must include spankings by his mother,
forgotten hatreds, devotions, father's dreams, sister's
prostitutions, old meals, and deprivations. At the
movies Smith boos the hero and heroine because the latter is a blonde. Rehumanizing the movie's iconography
means modifying the cultural values which the Renaissance articulated even before the Enlightenment objec-
tified Western culture. By Brooks's standards for a
heroine or hero (Langston Hughes, Big Bessie, Pepita,
Malcolm X, Medgar Evers, and the narrators in the ser-
mons), Satin-Legs fails, not because of an unwillingness
to confront a naturalistic world but in the ignorance
which keeps him from defining the world.[12] Understanding must precede confrontation.
    When Smith "squires" his "lady" to Joe's Eats his
action is just another prelude to sexual intercourse on
Sunday. "Squires" evokes the chivalric code of knights,
damsels, and jousts, but in the modern world the code
lacks meaning. Satin-Legs chooses a different prostitute, an ironic "lady." Each wears Queen Lace stockings
and "vivid shoes" without fronts and backs. Thick lip-
stick characterizes them all, as do Chinese fingernails
and earrings. The woman on this particular Sunday has

large breasts that comfort Smith in a way that standard
morality cannot serve: "He had no education / In quiet
arts of compromise. He would / Not understand your
counsels on control, nor / Thank you for your late trouble." Here the narrator's consciousness combines with
Smith's more closely than anywhere else since the poem's
beginning. Why is "education" ambiguous? Does it imply
the listener's hidden carnality which equals, possibly
even surpasses, Smith's? Does it suggest, as well, the
inability of this "you" to distinguish manners, the
standardization of values, from the values themselves?
As if to suspend her answers, the speaker describes the
serving methods at Joe's. Fish and chicken come on meat
platters; the coleslaw, macaroni, and candied yams come
on the side. Coffee and pie are also available. The
yams ("candied sweets") and the possibly sugared coffee
foreshadow the sexual act that ends the poem. The scene
appears through Satin-Legs's submerging consciousness as
the narrator creates a syntactic paradox. Although pa-
rentheses usually indicate understatement, dashes generally indicate stress. The speaker comments ironically
"(The end is — isn't it? — all that really matters.)"
She has shown, rather, that values characterize human
life.

"Still do I keep my look, my identity..." (*A Street
in Bronzeville*), a Petrarchan sonnet, clarifies a humanistic aesthetic by alliteration and plosive, by tension
between movement and inertia, and by juxtaposition of
heredity with environment. In general the poem associates a soldier's personal or individual style in
lovemaking, here ambiguously showing both violence and
grace, with the invariant self that appears regardless
of social class or life's experiences. Although this
self is untranslatable in terms of landscape and finally
in terms of this dead soldier's casket, the self does
become visible in forms and situations as different as
baseball and school. In the poem, depicting a soldier
who died during World War II, the surviving narrator
interprets the man's life, as empathy and love bind the
living with the dead. In thinking highly of her own
life-style, the narrator values his. The particular
therefore leads to the general, and the poem is less
about this soldier than about everyone. Two quatrains

and the sestet create the narrator's introspection, as
the first lines emphasize beauty.

With the "p" in "push of pain," the plosives in "pre-
cious prescribed pose" suggest harshness and abruptness
as well as death. The timeless narrator portrays a man
once alive and transitory. Can form bridge their two
worlds? She recalls his grief, his ambiguous "hatred
hacked." The latter is narrowness, the racial prejudice
which he withstood and overcame. Although the poem
states neither race nor color, he is Black. Like
Brooks's persona in "The Mother" (also in *Street*), he
lives in Bronzeville, a racial section of Chicago; he
is at the same time universal because here too the particular represents the general. The soldier waltzed
— showed grace — when confronting pain, inertia, and
prejudice. As with Brooks's Satin-Legs Smith, his environment determined his style. So war and dress vary
in artistic mode but not in human desire.

The second quatrain reinforces the dead soldier's
"pose," his earlier blending of heredity with environment: "No other stock / That is irrevocable, perpetual
/ And its to keep." The off-rhymes imply human indomi-
tability — "irrevocable, perpetual." The archetypal
need to create, to give form, differs as to social
class, for the soldier became his style "In castle or
in shack. / With rags or robes. Through good, nothing,
or ill." This last line stands out. Whereas ill is
lethargy and apathy, good is dynamism. As in Brooks's
"Sadie and Maud," living and losing surpasses not living
at all. By symbolizing life, style is the measure of
vertical and horizontal space: "And even in death a
body, like no other / On any *hill* or *plain* or crawling
cot" (my emphasis). Height and breadth end in alliteration and perplexity. Does a cot crawl, or do people?
And do people advance, regress? Brooks ended *Street in
Bronzeville* with "The Progress," a poem that portrays
well civilization's vulnerability. In "still do I keep
my look, my identity," however, the imaginative mind
is invulnerable. Having twisted, gagged, and died, the
soldier shows "the old personal art, the look. Shows
what / It showed at baseball. What it showed in school."

In sonnet 2 of "Children of the Poor" (*Annie Allen*),
the narrator more impersonally desires a humanistic aes-

thetic. For Brooks the verse reunited the formal with
the emotional and determined her future techniques.
Annie Allen showed her decision to create engaged narrators of the present rather than detached ones of the
past.[13] When appearing impersonal ("Bronzeville Mother...," "The Chicago *Defender* Sends a Man to Little
Rock"), her later speakers mask their actual involvement
and sincerity. Here the narrating mother relates directly her children's distressed inquiries. The children request not an easy life but a life with meaning,
since they see themselves as dehumanized objects, the
heirs of the nineteenth-century slaves who escaped safely to the northern lines. Social reality undermines the
children's religious belief, for what God could possibly
create such a world? The narrator herself, of course,
reflects this powerlessness rooted in social injustice,
since she ends by being neither alchemist, magician, nor
God. She is only a woman, signifying the writer who
creates her, whose planning and love (although great)
cannot redeem her children from autumn's cold. Here objectivity, irony, and polish deceive.[14]
    The poem opens with the parallelism and balance of
a rhetorical question: "What shall I give my children?
who are poor, / Who... / Who...."[15] Plosives emphasize
again the children's plight: "adjudged," "leastwise,"
"land," "demand," "velvety velour," "begged." Since the
narrator's listeners and readers live outside the sonnet, it nearly becomes a monologue written to them. Her
children, however, live in the poem's world of suffering, although outside its dramatic action. They speak
not through dialogue but through the narrator's memory.
Looking for fulfillment rather than for wealth, they are
less the individual than the type, and so is she. The
second quatrain blends the two viewpoints when her words
indirectly recreate theirs. With alliteration and metaphor she questions the fate of those "graven by a hand
/ Less than angelic, admirable or sure." Does she evoke
the myth of Hephaestus-Vulcan, craftsman, symbol of the
artist as well as the writer? What were his limitations? What are hers? Must she now rehumanize the
metaphor and myth as well as restore it? From "mode,
design, device" the narrator advances to grief and love,
but her world lacks magic, the alchemical stone. Her
poem ends in "autumn freezing" because she has come as

far as woman and man can. Having illuminated poverty,
she sees her poem end at that magic and divinity which
transcend craft. Even the writer and artist finally
must speak from a fallen world.

> My hand is stuffed with mode, design, device.
> But I lack access to my proper stone.
> And plenitude of plan shall not suffice
> Nor grief nor love shall be enough alone
> To ratify my little halves who bear
> Across an autumn freezing everywhere.

Brooks explores this idea further in "Langston
Hughes" (*Selected Poems*[16]), a short poem that combines
cheer and praise with images of speech and muscle. Here
the writer's "infirm profession" suggests human life,
but Hughes's bond with nature is ambivalent. While opposing its apparent determinism, he demonstrates its
aliveness. His name signifies historical Black/Man,
Black/Creative Writer, and Humanistic Man-Woman. The
poem blends synchrony with diachrony when the narrator's
final command "See" compels the reader to share the
writer's eternality. Although they are not exclusive,
these roles help the student to outline the poem into
four parts. The first (ll. 1-3) fuses writer, humanist,
and historical figure; the second (ll. 4-7) emphasizes
a quest for meaning; the third (ll. 8-15) develops the
theme of art; and the fourth (ll. 16-18) extends the
narrator's invitation to the reader. As the present
tense indicates continuity, Hughes synthesizes joy and
freedom. He combines integrity with quest (the "long
reach"), and his "strong speech" anthropomorphizes
language.[17] His "Remedial fears" and "Muscular tears"
relate him first to a cultural perception of Black suffering and second to a powerful compassion. His world
is an oxymoron, and his patterns of struggle, memory,
dramatic action, and celebration suggest Brooks's other
writings.

Since 1963 Brooks has portrayed the heroic self as
confronting nature's undeniable power. By choice her
Langston Hughes timelessly "Holds horticulture / In the
eye of the vulture." Having identified with his humanness in sections one and two, the narrator apocalypti-
cally fuses her vision with his in section three. As

the storyteller and artist, she represents Gwendolyn
Brooks, the creator in the externally historical world.
But that parallel (yet real) world can never be identi-
cal to the poem's. Brooks has given the speaker auton-
omy, an eternality like the Hughes in the title when
readers recreate the poem. She carefully establishes
the bond between narrator and persona; between persona,
narrator, and reader. All relate to wind imagery which
exposes at once man's internal and external worlds. The
complementary element of water appears within a framework that implies innovation and illumination. Here alliteration adds fluidity: "In the breath / Of the holo-
caust he [Hughes] / Is helmsman, hatchet, headlight."
The light imagery in the third section blends with the
one-word line "See" that begins the last section. The
narrator, en route, commands the reader to assume the
poet's role, the highest level of possibility. When she
calls writing poetry an "infirm profession," her sadness
occurs because the limitation (compression) appears
within the framing context of style, quest, being, sordidness, and passion. The poem ends by celebrating more
than the Harlem Renaissance of the 1920s; it represents
more than a writer and a man. It signifies the eternal
type which defines itself as freedom, courage, and
health: "See / One restless in the exotic time! and
ever, / Till the air is cured of its fever."

In "Boy Breaking Glass" (*In the Mecca*), the humanistic aesthetic is social and subjective. The poem pre-
sents art, the paradox of beauty, ugliness, destruction,
and creation; it fuses desecration with reverence. Complexity grows from allusions to the nineteenth century,
as the poem shows that loneliness and neglect reap hard-
ship and revenge. Brooks ironically contrasts the narrator who speaks artificially with the boy who speaks
somewhat neurotically. Congress, the Statue of Liberty,
the Hawaiian feast, and the Regency Room ironically
foreshadow the cliff, the snare, and the "exceeding
sun." Mental instability, animal imagery, and social
upheaval, in other words, form an unbreakable chain, and
Brooks illuminates this continuity against the background of the riots in America during the late 1960s.
    The poem has eight stanzas, two having six lines and
the remaining six having two. The narrator recognizes

both traditional and nontraditional worlds — what W.
E. B. Du Bois calls double consciousness.[18] In both
instances beauty concerns mythmaking. It approximates
Coleridge's primary imagination, the first symbolism and
vision of the Western world. But countermythmaking re-
news the primary myth so as to satisfy contemporary
need. When mythmaking declines to science (formalism)
the true artist rehumanizes craft; his or her new form
changes traditional aesthetics.
    The sensitive narrator loves the Black boy because
his art suits his socialization. Temporal and mental
space separate him from "us," the listener. His aesthetic, a paradox, is both revolutionary and reactionary, since it resurrects for the future that humanism
lost in the past: "I shall create! If not a note, a
hole. / If not an overture, a desecration." Destruction
and creation differ in degree rather than in kind, a degree that represents perspective.[19] Within a structure
implying racial and literary history, the narrator's
kind tone in the first and third stanzas complements the
boy's defiant tone in the second. Recalling the cargoes
in stanza three, the ship imagery in stanza four alludes
by interior monologue to his slave ancestry:

> "Don't go down the plank
> if you see there's no extension.
> Each to his grief, each to
> his loneliness and fidgety revenge.
> Nobody knew where I was and now I am no longer
>   there."

The narrator, however, speaks satirically from the viewpoint of traditional aesthetics: "The only sanity is a
cup of tea. / The music is in minors." Her artificial-
ity and delicacy muffle the "cry" of the first stanza as
well as the overture of the second. The gentility recalls Brooks's juxtaposition in "The Progress" of Jane
Austen's politeness with the carnage of World War II,
her masterful incongruity suggesting moral sordidness.
In "Boy Breaking Glass," however, politeness facilitates
detachment: "Each one other / is having different weather." The narrator indicates that the boy's destruction
of a window contrasts with her creation of the poem,
even though she understands his need for political
power, his expensive food, his lodging, and his freedom;

she knows that art explodes as well as beautifies. She
appreciates him

> Who has not Congress, lobster, love, luau
> the Regency Room, the Statue of Liberty,
> runs. A sloppy amalgamation.
> A mistake.
> A cliff.
> A hymn, a snare, and an exceeding sun.

because art must reveal the cultural self.

   Can understanding the type broaden scholars' readings
of Brooks's "The Chicago Picasso"? When reviewing *In
the Mecca,* Brian Benson praised the poem's "most starkly
beautiful description," and later William Hansell discussed Brooks's self-justification of art in the poem.[20]
The piece was written for the occasion of Mayor Richard
Daley's dedication of a statue, a bird-woman, to the
city on August 15, 1967. By contrasting the willingness to explore life with cowardice and insensitivity,
the poem resolves itself in the possibility of human
perception. Yet will is necessary to see. The stanzas,
nineteen lines altogether, present the nature of creativity (ll. 1-7), the paradox of its appreciation (ll.
8-15), and the narrator's resulting insight (ll. 16-
19). First comes the rhetorical question: "Does man
love Art?" By exiling one from comfort, home, and
beer, aesthetic experience necessitates pain and quest,
as balance and personification show: "Art hurts. Art
urges voyages —." Both artist and reader transcend
animalism ("belch, sniff, or scratch") imperfectly to
seek divinity.
   Humanism is paradox: "...we must cook ourselves and
style ourselves for Art, who / is a requiring courtesan." But a courtesan, a prostitute, sells herself to
the upper classes. How is Art a prostitute? Does it
make one abandon the private self for the public one?
Does the creator sacrifice selfhood and humanity? "We
do not," the speaker says, "hug the Mona Lisa." "Yes"
partially answers the last two questions, although pros-
titution here implies frailty more than corruption.
For the narrator's listeners, artifacts have autonomous
meaning. People ("We") admire romantic spectacles ("as-
tounding fountain"), traditional sculpture ("horse and

rider"), or standard animal ("lion"). We can bear any burden but our own humanity.

Do the people feel? The poem ends in cold. After the engaged "we," the viewpoint becomes again that of the detached narrator. Her objective poem has been "The Chicago Picasso" because Chicago is American and Picasso is Spanish — even if not parallel — the two representing the impersonalization of art in the Western (modern) world. To the narrator, form should include pain, rawness, and love. Like Brooks's speaker in "Second Sermon on the Warpland," this one shows tension between idealism and realism, Black and White, hatred and love, order and chaos. Resembling a woman and a bird, Picasso's cold steel can only imply flight, but the narrator represents the eternal need to soar, at least to sculpt and to write. Her imperative ending contrasts sharply with her interrogative beginning. Why has a statue now become a blossom to her? Here eternality depends less upon form (plants are transitory) than upon human perception and sincerity, the necessary qualities for a world facing sunset:

> Observe the tall cold of a Flower
> which is as innocent and as guilty,
> as meaningful and as meaningless as any
> other flower in the western field.

Brooks reaffirms the ontological self. With style and posture her personae withstand the science and barbarism of war or even death. Identity includes vertical and horizontal space as well as time. Living between animalism and divinity, the self seeks resolution; finding grief where magic disappears, it must be content with love. Whether by breaking glass or by creating an overture, separate people diversely experience a common end. To hear Brooks's universal voice, to transcend her form, the reader must ultimately be human.

A shorter version of this paper was read at the annual meeting of the Modern Language Association in December 1978.

[1]George E. Kent, "Preface: Gwen's Way," in *Report from Part I*, ed. Gwendolyn Brooks (Detroit: Broadside, 1972), p. 31.

[2]Unless noted differently, all citations of primary text refer to Gwendolyn Brooks, *The World of Gwendolyn Brooks* (New York: Harper and Row, 1971).

[3]In *Myth and Meaning* (New York: Schocken, 1977), Claude Lévi-Strauss views invariance as being the central unity in structures of human creativity.

[4]For convenience, "prostitute" appears here as a sensible term. "Woman" is inadequate because the poem implies looseness on the woman's part. Yet "looseness" is inexact for the same reason that "whore" would fail. The latter two terms imply the absence of dignity, which Brooks gives to this kind of woman in "a song in the front yard" (*World*, p. 12). Prostitute here is a generic rather than a moral category.

[5]John Lyons, *Noam Chomsky* (New York: Viking, 1970); Claude Lévi-Strauss, *The Savage Mind* (Chicago: Univ. of Chicago Press, 1966); idem, *Myth and Meaning;* Jacques Derrida, *Speech and Phenomena: And Other Essays on Husserl's Theory of Signs* (Evanston, Ill.: Northwestern Univ. Press, 1973).

[6]To observe the way Brooks's speakers function, see R. Baxter Miller, "'Define...the Whirlwind': IN THE MECCA — Urban Setting, Shifting Narrator, and Redemptive Vision," *Obsidian* 4 (Spring 1978): 19-31; and idem, "'My Hand Is Mode': Gwendolyn Brooks' Speakers and Their Stances," T.V. videotape for the University of Tennessee Division of Continuing Education, 1978.

[7]Miller, "'Define...the Whirlwind,'" pp. 19, 30.

[8]Andrew Marvell, *Selected Poetry* (New York: Signet, 1967), p. 76.

[9]"Re-search," as used here, linguistically demonstrates the problem of dehumanization. Etymologically the term implies subjective knowing, yet it has been reduced to meaning the verification of scientific data.

[10]Compare the female typology in "a song in the front yard," *World*, p. 12.

[11]This reading expands and applies the idea in Arthur P. Davis, "Gwendolyn Brooks: Poet of the Unheroic," *CLA Journal* 7 (December 1960): 114-25. The unheroism that Davis observes was probably true until 1963.

[12]See Miller, "'Define...the Whirlwind,'" where I observe this typology in the second half of *In the Mecca*.

[13]See Miller, "'My Hand Is Mode.'"

[14]Miller, "'Define...the Whirlwind,'" p. 26.

[15]George E. Kent, "The Poetry of Gwendolyn Brooks, Part II," *Black World* 20 (October 1971): 36-48. Kent considers the "Children of the Poor" sequence the most masterful description in poetry of the Black mother's dilemma and one of the most memorable, as well as rhythmical, pieces in English.

[16]*Selected Poems* (New York: Harper and Row, 1963), p. 123.

[17]Compare the theme of reaching (questing) in "Life for my child is simple, and is good," *World,* p. 104.

[18]In "The Achievement of Gwendolyn Brooks," *CLA Journal* 16

(Fall 1972): 23-31, Houston A. Baker, Jr., .says well that Brooks's poetry demonstrates White form and Black content. Are these terms difficult to define? Are they mutually exclusive?

[19]In "'Define...the Whirlwind,'" my explication of *In the Mecca,* I describe it as a volume that "seeks to balance the sordid realities of urban life with an imaginative process of reconciliation and redemption" (p. 20).

[20]Respectively, "Review of *In the Mecca,*" *CLA Journal* 13 (December 1969): 203; "Aestheticism versus Political Militancy in Gwendolyn Brooks' 'The Chicago Picasso' and 'The Wall,'" *CLA Journal* 17 (September 1973): 11-15. See also R. Baxter Miller, *Langston Hughes and Gwendolyn Brooks: A Reference Guide* (Boston: G. K. Hall, 1978), p. xxiv.

Contributors

Richard K. Barksdale has a Ph.D. from Harvard. He is advisory editor to *CLA Journal* and *Black American Literature Forum,* consultant to NEH, and coeditor (with Keneth Kinnamon) of *Black Writers in America: A Comprehensive Anthology* (1971). His most recent book is *Langston Hughes: The Poet and His Critics* (1977). He is associate dean of the Graduate School at the University of Illinois-Urbana.

Alice Childress, a graduate of the Radcliffe Institute, is author of *Gold through the Trees, Trouble in Mind, Like One in the Family, Wedding Band, a Hero Ain't Nothing but a Sandwich,* and *Wine in the Wilderness.* She won an Obie Award (1956) and an achievement award from New York National Business and Professional Women (1975). Recently she has written a television drama on the life of Fannie Lou Hamer.

Chester J. Fontenot, Jr., is advisory editor to *Black American Literature Forum* and has been general editor of *WATU: A Cornell Journal of Black Writing.* Holding the Ph.D. from the University of California, Irvine, he is editor of *Writing about Black Literature* (1976) and author of *Franz Fanon: Language as a God Gone Astray* (1979). Chairman of the MLA Forum on Black Literature, he is associate professor of English at the University of Illinois-Urbana.

Michael S. Harper, a graduate of the writer's workshop at the University of Iowa, is author of *Dear John: Dear Coltrane* (1970), *History Is Your Own Heartbeat* (1971), *History as Apple Tree* (1972), *Song: I Want a Witness* (1972), *Debridement* (1973), *Nightmare Begins Responsibility* (1975), and *Images of Kin* (1977). He has been visiting professor at Reed, Yale, and Harvard. His honors include awards from the National Institute of Arts and Letters (1972), the Black Academy of Arts and

Letters (1972), the Guggenheim Foundation (1976), and
the National Endowment for the Arts (1977). He is
chairman of creative writing and professor of English
at Brown University.

Trudier Harris, a graduate of the Ph.D. program at
Ohio State University, has presented numerous papers
across the country. Her stories and scholarly studies
have appeared in *Southern Humanities Review, BOP*
(Brown), *CLA Journal, Black American Literature Forum,
Mississippi Folklore Register,* and *MELUS.* She is now
writing a book on the typology of the Black domestic,
and is associate professor of English at the University
of North Carolina at Chapel Hill.

George E. Kent earned his Ph.D. at Boston University.
He has been advisory editor to *Obsidian, CLA Journal,
Black American Literature Forum,* and *Black Books Bulle-
tin.* The author of numerous publications and antholo-
gized articles, he has written *Blackness and the Adven-
ture of Western Culture: Literary Essays and Research
Articles* (1972). During 1977–1978 he was a senior NEH
fellow. Professor of English at the University of Chicago, he is completing the first biography of Gwendolyn
Brooks.

R. Baxter Miller, associate professor of English and
director of the Black literature program at the University of Tennessee, earned the Ph.D. at Brown University.
His articles and reviews have been widely published.
He is the author of *Langston Hughes and Gwendolyn
Brooks: A Reference Guide* (1978), and has been advisory
editor to *WATU* and *Obsidian,* as well as guest editor for
a special issue of *Black American Literature Forum* on
Langston Hughes.